Complete Book of
Sewing Techniques

Complete Book of
Sewing Techniques

More Than 30 Essential Sewing Techniques for You to Master

Wendy Gardiner

COMPANIONHOUSE
BOOKS

COMPLETE BOOK OF SEWING TECHNIQUES

CompanionHouse Books™ is an imprint of Fox Chapel Publishers International Ltd.

Project Team
Editorial Director: Christopher Reggio
Editor: Colleen Dorsey
Copy Editor: Laura Taylor
Art Director: Mary Ann Kahn
Designer: Wendy Reynolds
Index: Jay Kreider

ISBN 978-1-62008-236-2

Library of Congress Cataloging-in-Publication Data

Names: Gardiner, Wendy, author.
Title: Complete book of sewing techniques / Wendy Gardiner.
Description: Mount Joy : CompanionHouse Books, 2017. | Includes
   bibliographical references and index.
Identifiers: LCCN 2017028427 | ISBN 9781620082362 (pbk. : alk. paper)
Subjects: LCSH: Sewing.
Classification: LCC TT705 .G37 2017 | DDC 646.2—dc23
LC record available at https://lccn.loc.gov/2017028427

Fox Chapel Publishing
903 Square Street
Mount Joy, PA 17552

Fox Chapel Publishers International Ltd.
7 Danefield Road, Selsey (Chichester)
West Sussex PO20 9DA, U.K.

www.facebook.com/companionhousebooks

Printed and bound in Singapore
20 19 18 17   2 4 6 8 10 9 7 5 3 1

Contents

Sewing Essentials

SEWING MACHINES

There is a huge range of sewing machines available today, ranging from basic models that do straight and zigzag stitch, to computerized embroidery machines that can stitch beautiful embroidery designs that you have customized yourself.

A sewing machine helps you to stitch faster, creating neat, even stitching time after time. Using the correct feet (see page 13) also helps with different types of sewing, whether it is inserting a zipper or creating perfectly formed buttonholes every time. Using different stitches that are built into the sewing machine enables you to embellish and customize by adding decorative stitching, trims, and fringe.

HOW THEY WORK

Electronic models stitch automatically when pressure is applied to the foot pedal – the heavier the pressure, the faster the machine stitches. Stitch choice, length, and width are chosen by changing the direction of dials or buttons, usually located on the front of the machine. They might also have a small LCD screen to show selections made.

Computerized models are fully automated – they automatically set the correct stitch tension, length, and width for the stitch you have chosen on the LCD touch screen. The screen also displays the recommended foot, and the option to change the stitch length or width, etc., to suit your own preferences. For instance, you may select a straight stitch, but want to increase the stitch length to maximum in order to make a gathering stitch. The automatic tension means that you can sew a single layer of flimsy fabric as evenly as multi-layers of denim or fleece. Computerized models also have a variety of embroidery designs and alphabets built in.

Stitch dials

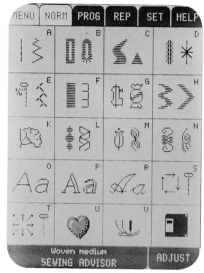

An LCD display

CHOOSING A NEW SEWING MACHINE

Which type of sewing machine you buy will depend on budget, type of sewing, and personal preference. However, always buy the best you can afford, even if it has more features than you need at the moment—you can grow in to them. The following are a few basic guidelines to consider when choosing a new machine:

- Try out different models in your budget range to see how they sew different weights and types of fabric. Take your own fabric samples to try.
- Check the ease of threading both top thread and bobbin. Can the bobbin be wound with thread without unthreading the top thread and needle? Useful if a new bobbin is needed in the middle of a seam! Drop-in bobbins are less awkward than front-loading (or rotary hook) bobbins.
- Most modern machines have snap-on feet, which makes changing feet for different sewing techniques much easier. Check what feet are included in the basic price and what optional extras are available. Essentials are straight stitch, buttonhole, zipper, blind-hem, darning/free motion, appliqué.
- Look for a variable stitch speed which allows you to control how fast or slow you stitch. This is very important when stitching around tricky curves and corners or applying appliqué.
- If you intend to sew soft furnishings and other large projects, check the size of the throat space between the body of the machine and the needle. Bigger is better in order to fit large quantities of fabric through. Equally, a wide flatbed surface helps guide fabric. Some machines have an optional extension table.
- If you intend to carry your machine to workshops, check the weight and portability. What type of cover does it have? Note that computerized machines are much heavier than electronic machines.
- Ask about warranty, servicing, and repair facilities. Many manufacturers offer a 3- to 5-year warranty.
- Ask about courses, workshops, and after-sales service. Many manufacturers offer tutorials as part of the purchase price.
- How easy will it be to update a computerized model? Technology continues to advance, bringing new developments and stitch choices—can your preferred model be updated?

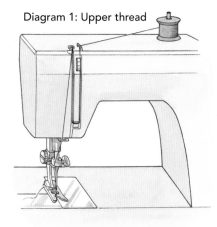
Diagram 1: Upper thread

THREADING

Each sewing machine looks slightly different depending on the model and manufacturer. However, the main principles are the same on all. Check your user's manual to determine where the relevant features are on your model.

Upper thread

Most machines have one or two upper-thread pins on which the thread spool is placed; these may be vertical or horizontal. Which way round to place the spool (with thread coming over the top or from under the spool) is important because it can affect the way the machine stitches, so check your user's manual. Once the thread is on the pin, add a spool holder to keep the spool from bouncing up and down the pin when it revolves (which will cause uneven stitching or broken threads). The thread is then taken from the spool, through a thread guide on the top of the machine, down, then up through tension disks before being fed behind a hook on the needle column and then threaded from the front to the back of the needle (diagram 1).

Bobbins

Although you can buy universal bobbins, it is preferable to use those that are supplied with the machine because some models get temperamental if using other types of bobbin. Bobbins can be wound with the same thread as the upper thread or with a special bobbin fill if doing machine embroidery or lots of appliqué (bobbin fill is finer, making it ideal for heavily concentrated stitch areas). Place the bobbin on the bobbin winder pin (at the front or the side of the machine) and push the pin into the wind position. On modern machines this disengages the needle and allows you to wind bobbins without unthreading the upper thread (check your user's manual). Use the bobbin winder for general sewing thread to ensure an evenly wound bobbin. If it is too loosely wound or uneven, it may cause the bobbin to jam when sewing, which can cause broken or uneven stitching. (If you are using speciality threads for a decorative finish, hand-wind them onto the bobbin and then stitch slowly.) Clean the bobbin area frequently using the brush provided in the tool kit to prevent fluff build up (which can jam the machine).

Winding a bobbin

STARTING TO STITCH

It is preferable to bring up the bobbin thread before you start to stitch to prevent the threads tangling at the start of a seam. To raise the bobbin thread, turn the fly wheel by hand to lower and raise the needle. As the upper thread comes back up, pull it from behind the needle to bring up the bobbin thread loop and then pull both together to create a 2–3 in (5–8 cm) thread tail.

Stitch length

An average stitch length for medium-weight fabric is 2.5–3 mm or 10–12 spi (stitches per inch). Stitch length is altered by a dial on electronic machines, or by tapping the increase/decrease points on the LCD screen of a computerized model. There will be a minimum and maximum stitch length – minimum is used to stitch on the spot and maximum for basting or gathering stitches. Shorter stitch lengths are used for finer fabrics, and longer stitch lengths are used for sewing bulkier fabrics.

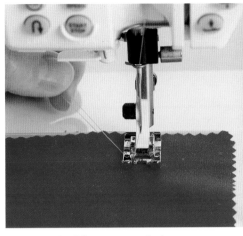

To ensure the fabric is not pulled down into the throat plate and to prevent threads tangling at the start of stitching, hold the thread tails at the back when making the first few stitches.

STITCH LENGTH GUIDE	
Fabric	**Stitch length**
Very lightweight fabrics – voiles/organza/chiffon	2–2.5 mm or 10–12 spi
General sewing cottons, poly cottons, etc.	2.5–3 mm or 8–10 spi
Medium-weight wools, worsteds, gabardine	3–3.5 mm or 7–8 spi
Heavyweight wools, tweeds, fleece	3.5–5 mm or 5–7 spi

HELPFUL HINT:
Test stitch the length and width on a sample made up of the same number of layers and interfacings, etc. Adjust the length/width as necessary to achieve an even, straight row of stitching.

Stitch width

The stitch width is only applicable on stitches that have a sideways element, such as a zigzag stitch or decorative stitches. Adjust with the dial or LCD screen as for length, reducing or increasing to suit the fabric weight and stitch choice.

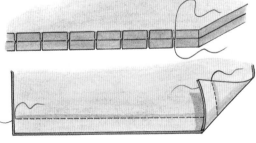

Stitch tension is correct when the upper thread shows on the top of the fabric and the bobbin thread shows on the underside. The two threads are interlocked between the fabric layers.

GUIDE TO OTHER MACHINE PARTS

Flywheel – Also known as the hand wheel. Turn it to lower and raise the needle, step by step.

Needle – Sewing machine needles have a flat surface on one side of the shaft. For most machines, this is placed in the needle column facing to the back. To secure the needle in position, tighten the screw with the screwdriver provided in the tool kit.

Presser foot – This is used to help keep the fabric in position as it is fed through when being stitched. Snap-on feet are easy to remove and replace. The presser foot is lifted or lowered using a lever on the side or back of the foot column or by a computerized button.

Feed dogs – Positioned under the presser foot, these raised, jagged edges move back and forth when the machine is in use in order to feed the fabric as it is being stitched. Lowering the feed dogs disengages them and thus enables you to move the fabric in any direction as it is being stitched.

Throat plate (or needle plate) – This metal plate has a central hole which fits over the feed dogs and provides a space for the needle to go down and pick up the bobbin thread. The different markings are used as a guide for seam width. Alternative throat plates with smaller apertures are available for some models.

Flat bed and free arm – These are the terms for the sewing surface. The flat bed usually incorporates the tool kit/machine accessory case which can be removed to make the sewing surface. The free arm is a thinner base used when sewing small items, such as cuffs or trouser hems.

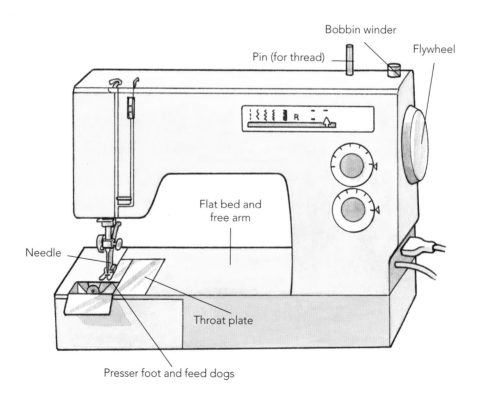

Bobbin winder

Pin (for thread)

Flywheel

Flat bed and free arm

Needle

Throat plate

Presser foot and feed dogs

Presser feet

Every sewing machine is provided with a basic range of feet which help sew specific techniques, such as a general purpose foot, zipper foot, and buttonhole foot. Other feet are usually available as optional extras. Each has different widths, grooves underneath to move smoothly over concentrated stitch areas, or hooks and angles through which trims, piping, etc., can be fed.

All-purpose foot – The most frequently used foot, ideal for straight stitching.

Zipper foot – These can vary in appearance, but all are designed to allow stitching close to the zipper teeth.

Buttonhole foot – These vary from model to model. Some have a slot to insert a button at the back. The underside has deep grooves to allow it to glide over dense stitching.

Embroidery/appliqué/satin stitch foot – Usually clear plastic, a wide groove on the underside helps the foot glide over concentrated stitching.

Blind hem foot – Used to machine stitch blind hems, the foot has a metal guide against which the folded fabric is fed.

Overcasting foot – Designed to stitch at the edge of the fabric, it has a wire brush on the underside to prevent the fabric edge from rolling or puckering.

Walking foot – Although large and cumbersome to look at, this foot helps feed fabric layers through evenly and is ideal for fabrics with a pile such as fur, or for accurately matching plaids and quilting several layers.

All-purpose and zipper feet

Walking foot

Embroidery foot, blind hem foot and overcasting foot

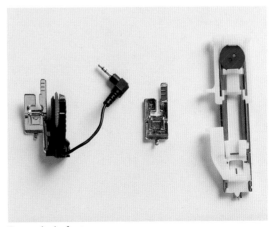

Buttonhole feet

SERGERS

Sergers (also known as overlockers) are ideal for fast sewing because they stitch, trim fabric from the seam allowance, and finish all at the same time. They use between 2–8 threads to complete the process, depending on the stitch technique and type of serger. The most common machines have three or four threads while the top of the range have eight thread positions and the option to cover stitch as well as serge. Serged seams are flexible, making them ideal for stretchy fabrics, sportswear, and lingerie.

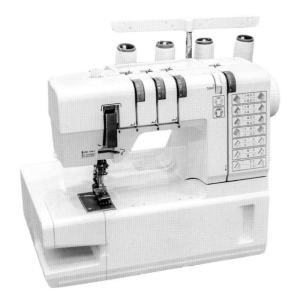

HOW SERGERS WORK

Sergers do not have bobbins, but have one or two needles and two loopers instead. The needles stitch straight rows of stitching, while the upper and lower loopers form the overcast stitch along the cut edge, interlocking at the very edge. All four are threaded through individual thread tensions with cones or cops of thread held on pins at the back of the machine. It is often necessary to thread in a specific sequence in order to make the machine stitch properly (check your user's manual for threading guide).

Sergers also have cutting blades positioned to the right of the needle, so that when the machine is operated, the fabric edge is cut before it continues to feed under the foot to be stitched and overlocked. The blades can be lowered to disengage them if desired.

Serger cones

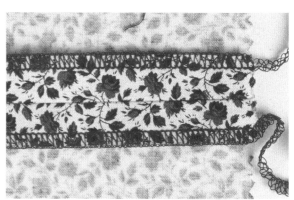

Fabric that has been overlocked

Modern sergers also have differential feed, which means that they evenly feed fabric layers at the same time, avoiding overstretched or puckered seams.

Sergers can be used simply to finish seams quickly and efficiently, or to create decorative finishes when using the special feet available, such as creating a rolled hem, gathering, attaching bindings, and piping. Although feet and needles carry out the same function as on sewing machines, they are rarely interchangeable.

Serger thread is usually finer and comes on large cones or cops (sometimes called bobbins, but not to be confused with sewing machine bobbins) because serging uses far more thread than a sewing machine. If using speciality threads, use them in the loopers which have larger-eyed needles.

A blade cuts the fabric before stitching

STARTING TO STITCH

Always test the stitching on a sample before working on the main project. Start stitching before the fabric is fed through in order to create a chain of stitches 3–5 in (8–10 cm) long. Then, holding the chain at the back of the machine, feed the fabric under the foot (which can be left down or raised to start). Always have the blade at its highest point when starting (turn the hand wheel by hand to raise it). At the seam end, continue stitching for a further 3–5 in (8–10 cm) to create another chain of stitches. Use a bodkin (large-eyed needle) to thread this chain back through the overlocked edge.

HELPFUL HINT:
Before changing or removing needles, place fabric under the presser foot so that the needle cannot accidentally drop down through the throat plate.

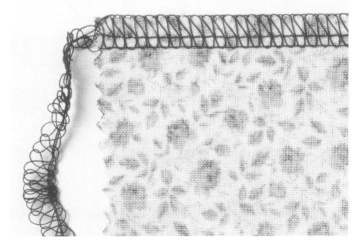

Leave a thread tail at the end

THE DIFFERENT PARTS OF THE SERGER

Needles – A three-thread serger has one needle whereas a four-thread machine has two needles, and a five-thread may have three needles. A three-thread machine stitches a straight line and overlocks the edge in one pass which is generally only used for seam finishing. The four-thread serger with two needles stitches a seam plus a parallel straight line and overlocked edge making it a stronger combination, useful for complete garment or project construction. Needles can be removed if the stitch technique doesn't require all needles in operation, as in flat locking which requires one needle only.

Loopers – The function of the loopers is to form the overlocked stitching at the fabric edge. The looper threads go through their own thread guides, which take them under the needle plate. Threading the loopers can be tricky. The lower looper thread forms the stitching on the underside of the work and the upper looper thread forms the stitching on the top.

Thread guide – Each is usually color coded so that the correct needle or looper thread trail is easier to follow. Cones are placed on pins at the back of the machine and should then be covered with nets (provided in the tool kit) to prevent threads unravelling from the cones unevenly. The thread guide at the back can be raised when in use and lowered for storage.

Thread tensions – Some models have automatic thread tensions on all threads, others have dials to alter the tensions individually. Those with dials usually have shaded or marked optimum tension settings. Tensions may need to be altered when using different stitch techniques or stitching very fine or very bulky fabric. If the looper stitches do not interlock on the fabric edge, the upper looper tension may be too tight, or lower looper too loose. Tighten and loosen the tensions a little at a time.

Stitch selector – As with sewing machines, sergers have stitch options in order to create different finishes. Your user's manual will advise on any tension alterations and the recommended foot and needles.

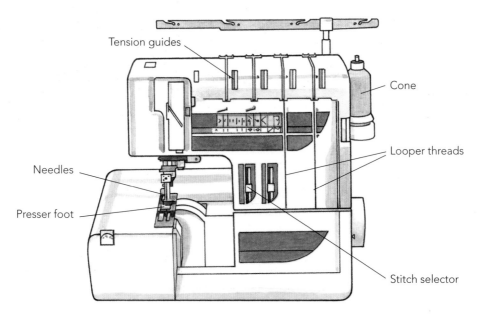

Tension guides

Cone

Needles

Presser foot

Looper threads

Stitch selector

FABRICS

There is a huge range of fabrics available for dressmaking, crafts, and soft furnishings. Which to use and when depends on the type of project, whether you want something bold and dramatic or classic and understated. Most important is to use the right type and weight of fabric. Following is a list of the common fabric types and their uses.

Selection of lightweight fabrics

LIGHTWEIGHT FABRICS

Many different fabrics are available in lightweight varieties, including cottons, voiles, linens, silks, woolens, and poly cotton blends. Most are stable, woven fabrics that are easy to sew. Cotton, linen, silk, and wool are made from natural fibers, which are often mixed with man-made fibers to create fabrics that are stronger and more wrinkle-resistant.

Use all-purpose thread and finish seams with overcast stitch, zigzag stitch, or pinking shears. Pure cottons and linens can be pressed with a hot iron. For silks, wools, and mixed-fiber fabrics, always use a press cloth and medium to hot iron. Use a 10–12 (70–80) universal needle.

Linen and linen-mix fabrics

Common fabric types

Batiste – Lightweight, soft, and sheer, batiste can be made in cotton, wool, or synthetic fibers. Used for underlinings, quilt backing, and heirloom sewing.

Chambray – Similar in appearance to denim, chambray is normally cotton, although sometimes mixed with other fibers. Used for shirts and childrenswear.

Cheesecloth – A cotton fabric, loosely woven with a slightly crinkled surface. Used for crafts, casual gypsy-style tops, and other fashion items.

Chiffon – A light, drapable sheer fabric that can be pure silk or synthetic. Used for blouses, over-skirts, and wraps.

Cottons, polyester/cotton – Very versatile, easy to sew, and available in a huge color range, both in plains and prints. Used for summer clothing, craft projects, and quilting.

Cotton lawn – Lightweight and crisp to handle. Used for christening gowns, heirloom stitching, and linings.

Eyelet embroidery (broderie anglaise) – Traditionally a cotton fabric, it has a light self-colored pattern which incorporates stitched eyelets. Used for childrenswear, summer tops, full skirts, and nightwear.

Gingham – A check fabric, usually cotton. Used for dresses, blouses, craft projects, and café-style curtains.

Georgette – A sheer fabric, similar to chiffon but made with crêpe yarns for a more dense finish. Used for blouses and wraps.

Linen – Easily wrinkled, linens can be very lightweight (handkerchief linen) or medium-weight when mixed with other fibers (linen blends) which makes them more wrinkle-resistant and stable.

Handkerchief linen is used for tops and table linen. Linen and linen blends are used for smart suits, dresses, trousers, and jackets.

Muslin – A plain woven, inexpensive cream-colored cotton fabric. Different weights are available. Used for quilting or making toiles (test garments).

Muslin gauze – A lightweight, plain weave fabric. Used for crafts, lightweight curtains, and interfacings.

Organza/organdie – Slightly crisper than chiffon, organza is also sheer and often made of polyester or silk. Used for wraps and crisp blouses.

Polyester, polyester crêpe de chine, viscose, rayon – Man-made, these fabrics can range from light to medium weight. They look and feel like natural fiber fabrics, but with greater strength, wrinkle-resistance, and wearability. However, polyesters do fray easily so seam finishing is crucial. Used in the same way as silks, cottons, and wools, depending on weight.

Poplin – Slightly heavier and crisper than cotton lawn, poplin is woven with a fine horizontal rib. Used for summerwear and childrenswear.

Seersucker – Lightweight, usually cotton, seersucker has alternating stripes that are puckered and crinkled. Used for lightweight jackets and tops.

Silks – There are many silk varieties, including crêpe de chine, raw silk, shantung, thai silk, silk noil, china silk, polyester, viscose, and rayon silks. Raw silks, shantung, and noils have some surface texture and shading. Treat as a pile fabric and use "with nap" layouts. Silks can range from light to medium weight. Used for dressmaking and luxury soft furnishings. China silk is used for linings.

Taffeta/moiré taffeta – Originally made from silk, taffetas can also be polyester. They have a

Eyelet embroidery (broderie anglaise)

crisp finish and shiny surface. Moiré taffeta has a "watermark" pattern. Used for eveningwear, wraps, and bridalwear.

Tulle – Made from silk, nylon, or other man-made fibers, tulle is a fine net. Used for bridal veils and fancy-dress costumes.

Voile – A sheer, lightweight plain weave fabric, some have iridescent fibers for added shimmer. Used for lightweight drapes and summer wraps.

MEDIUM-WEIGHT FABRICS

These include fabrics suitable for dressmaking, craft, and soft furnishings such as wools, wool mixes, heavier silks, satins, and cottons with textured weave. Most are easy-to-sew, stable woven fabrics.

Use all-purpose thread and finish seams with overcast stitch, zigzag stitch, or bound seams. Alternatively, sew with special seams such as flat fell or French (see Seams, page 74). Always use a press cloth and steam. Allow to cool before handling. Use size 12 (80) needles.

Selection of medium-weight fabrics

Common fabric types

Angora, alpaca – Luxury soft wool fabrics: angora comes from goat hair and alpaca from llama. Angora is often mixed with other fibers to create a woolen cloth. Used for knitwear and woolen coating.

Challis – Woven with a crêpe yarn to give an all-over crinkled surface. Wool challis is a luxury fabric, it breathes well, and wrinkles very little.

Often printed with paisley or floral designs. Used for dresses, jackets, and A-line or full skirts.

Chintz – A cotton fabric that is closely woven and has a glazed finished. Used for crafts, table linen, and soft furnishings.

Corduroy – Has a sheared rib surface and can be pure cotton or a mix of fibers. Rib size can vary from narrow baby cord to thick elephant cord.

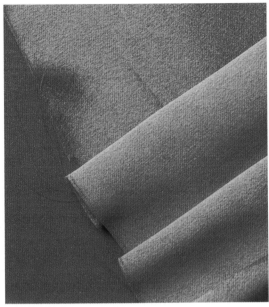

Crêpe back satin

Denim fabrics

Use "with nap" layouts. Used for trousers, jackets, vests, etc.

Crêpe back satin – Also known as satin back crêpe, this is a double-sided fabric with twisted crêpe weave on one side and a smooth, shiny satin on the other. Used for evening wear, bridal wear, smart trousers, jackets, and dresses.

Damask – Traditionally made from linen or cotton on a jacquard loom to produce a self pattern. Used for table linen and home furnishings.

Denim – A twill weave fabric that is now available in many different colors and weights. The very distinctive twill weave is created by a colored warp and white weft. Used for trousers, jackets, and skirts, depending on the weight.

Drill – A strong twill weave and heavier-weight cotton. Canvas is a similar fabric. Used for outdoor and hardwearing items.

Dupion – Has a thick uneven texture created by two fibers of silk woven together. Can also be made from synthetic fibers. Used for lightweight jackets, dresses, and tops.

Flannel – Can be plain or twill weave, both having a soft brushed surface on one or both sides. Used for jackets, suits, skirts, and trousers.

Gabardine – A close twill weave gives the distinctive surface pattern. Made from a variety of fibers and wool blends, it is water-repellent and hardwearing. Used for suits, trousers, skirts, jackets, and coats.

Satin/duchesse satin – A high sheen, smooth fabric. Use "with nap" layout to prevent unwanted shading. Duchesse satin has a very high luster. Used for bridal and evening wear.

Wool crêpe – Has a twisted weave which creates surface texture. Different weights and varieties are available, better qualities are more wrinkle-resistant. Crêpe can shrink when laundered, so pre-shrink before cutting out. Used for suits, tailored skirts and trousers, jackets, and dresses.

HEAVYWEIGHT FABRICS

Many fabric types have heavyweight varieties, such as woolens, tweeds, bouclés, and fleece. Many also have a one-way sheen or pile, such as cashmere, so always use the "with nap" layout. Use a press cloth and minimal steam, and press from the wrong side whenever possible. For very fluffy, hairy fabrics, use a towel as a pressing surface to prevent the pile flattening when pressed. Trim the pile from the seam allowances to reduce bulk. Use lining fabrics for facings to avoid unnecessary bulk at collars, cuffs, etc. Use size 10–12 (70–80) universal needles and medium- to heavyweight interfacings. Use sew-in interfacings on pile fabrics.

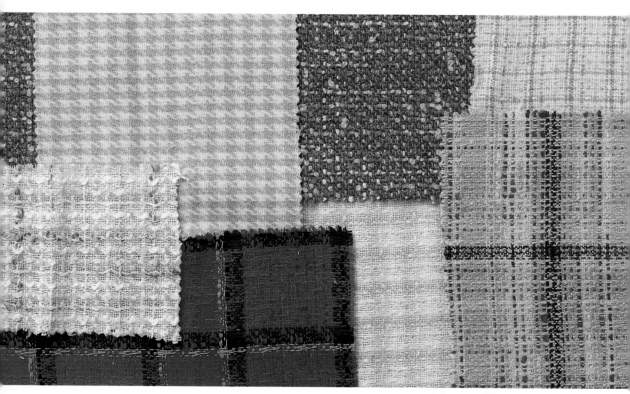

Selection of heavyweight fabrics

Common fabric types

Boiled wool – A felted knitted fabric. Create your own by machine washing and drying a loosely woven knit wool. Fabric will shrink by 40–50% in both directions. Used for jackets, fitted tops, and coats.

Bouclé – Can be knitted or woven, usually with a dull textural, thick, nobbly surface. Used for jackets, vests, and coats.

Brocade – Incorporates a jacquard design of flowers, leaves, or geometric patterns to create a raised surface contrast or color. Used for bridal- or eveningwear and table linen.

Camel hair – Woven from the under hair of a camel, it is often mixed with sheep's wool, for greater durability. It is a luxury fabric with a distinctive soft yellow color. Used for coats and jackets.

Cashmere – Made from the hair of Kashmir goats, this very fine, soft fabric is comfortable to wear. Cashmere can be knitted or woven. Used for coats, scarves, and sweaters.

Chenille – Soft to touch, with a raised surface texture. Good drapability but inclined to stretch. Fully interface with a fusible interfacing. Used for vests, jackets, loose tunic tops, and bathrobes.

Fleece – Very versatile and easy to sew, available in many colors and designs. Usually polyester, easy care and wear. Use a slightly larger-than-usual seam allowance to help feed the fabric evenly. No finishing needed. Used for jackets, vests, and coats.

Herringbone – Has a twill weave with a distinctive pattern like the backbone of a herring. Used for jackets, coats, and suits.

Mohair – Noted for its hairy texture, mohair is a plain weave fabric produced from the fibers of the angora goat. Frequently mixed with wool. Used for coats and jackets.

Tartan – A check, twill weave fabric with a specific check pattern. Careful layout needed to match fabric pattern. Used for kilts, skirts, and trousers.

Tartan fabrics

Tweed – *Scottish, Irish, Harris, and Donegal* – Traditional tweeds are thick woolen fabrics with a distinct woven pattern, named after the area of origin. Modern tweed is produced in a wider range of colors and designs. Used for coats, jackets, and smart suits.

Worsted – Made from tightly woven woolen yarns, it is hardwearing and usually high quality. Used for suits, coats, and upholstery.

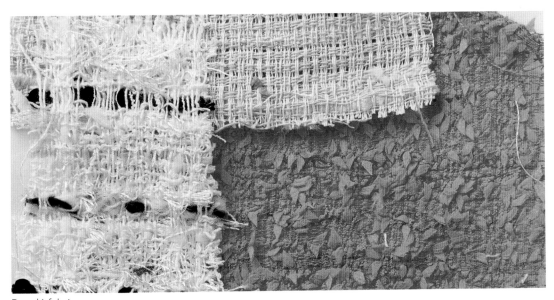

Bouclé fabric

KNIT FABRICS

Knits can be light- to heavyweight depending on the fabric type. They have definite stretch and can be used for close-fitting garments, sportswear, and casual wear. Use ballpoint needles and woven interfacings that can stretch. Stay stitch curved seams. Use stay tape at the neck and armholes to prevent unwanted stretch through prolonged wear. Use zigzag or stretch stitches that allow the fabric to stretch, even when sewn.

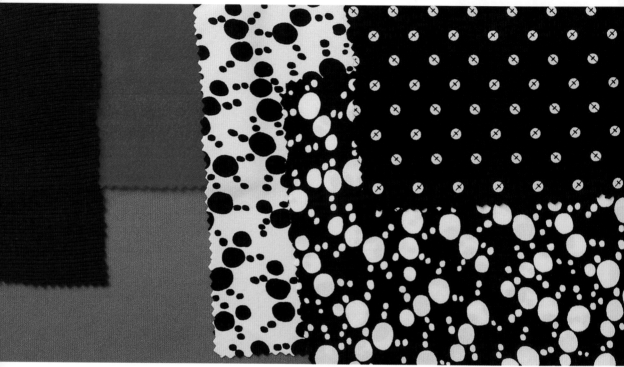

Selection of knit fabrics

Common fabric types

Cotton jersey – A fine, lightweight knit fabric which drapes well and is wrinkle-resistant. Orginally only cotton, many other soft-knitted fabrics are called jersey. Used for T-shirts, casual dresses, and sportswear.

Double knit – A very stable fabric, with vertical ribs on both sides. Available in a wide color range. Used for sportswear and casual suits.

Lycra and Spandex – Lycra is the trade name for Spandex. This man-made elastic fiber is often combined with other fibers to add stretch. Mixed with cotton it is matte, mixed with nylon it is shiny. Good for very close-fitting, active wear. Used for exercise wear, swimwear, and lingerie.

Lamé – Contains a mixture of metallic yarns and can be found in tricot-backed lamé and tissue lamé. It is a fragile fabric which tears easily. Avoid pressing. Used for loose tops, eveningwear, trims, and appliqués.

Stretch velour – Sometimes mixed with Lycra, velour is similar to velvet but with a tightly woven short cut pile. Used for sportswear, robes, and kaftans.

SPECIALITY FABRICS

These range from synthetic leathers and furs to natural fiber luxury fabrics. Many have piles and textured surfaces so always use "with nap" layout. Avoid pressing with steam, which can flatten the pile, and use a soft towel or velvet board as a pressing surface.

Common fabric types

Faux fur, fun fur – All have pile, some very long, others very short. Use "with nap" layouts and reduce bulk in the seam allowances by trimming the pile. Use a long stitch length and wider seam allowance to help evenly feed the fabric as it is sewn. Used for coats, jackets, and soft furnishings.

Synthetic suede/leather – Similar in look and feel to their natural counterparts, they rarely need finishing. Avoid pins, which will leave holes. Varieties include faux suede, suedette, ultra suede, leatherette, and pleather. Use a Teflon™ or coated presser foot to help glide over the fabric. Used for jackets, coats, skirts, trousers, and soft furnishings.

Velvet – A luxury fabric with a pile that can be made from cotton, silk, or man-made fibers. It can be light- or heavyweight. Varieties include panne, chiffon, velveteen, sculptured, and devoré. Devoré has a pattern created by parts of the pile being cut or burned away to reveal the backing. Velvet layers can "walk"; when sewing, use a walking foot or double pin and baste. Make sure the nap/pile is running in the same direction on all pieces. Used for eveningwear, jackets, trousers, and wraps.

HANDLING FABRICS

Having chosen the fabric, the next step is to cut it out, ready to sew. However, there are guidelines you should follow to ensure success. These include understanding and using the fabric grain and using special techniques to sew specialty fabrics.

Grain lines

All woven fabrics have a grain (diagram 1). The grain determines the amount of stretch in the fabric. The lengthwise or straight grain runs parallel with the selvages (side edges). It has the least stretch and therefore most garment pieces are placed with the lengthwise grain running vertically down the pattern piece. The crosswise grain is at right angles to the lengthwise grain and runs from selvage to selvage. It has slightly more give than the lengthwise grain, thus most pattern pieces are laid on the fabric with the crosswise grain going around the body. The bias is any diagonal direction. The true bias runs at a 45-degree angle to the lengthwise grain. Fabric is at its most stretchy along the bias.

Diagram 1: Grain lines

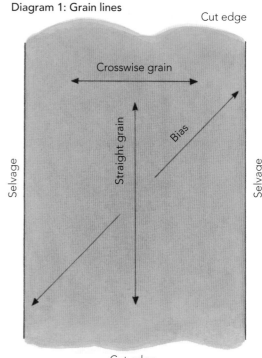

Cut edge

Crosswise grain

Straight grain

Bias

Selvage

Selvage

Cut edge

Sewing tips for specialty fabrics
General

- Use sharp shears to cut out. Use serrated shears when cutting silks or very fine fabrics. The serrated blades will grip the fabric as it is cut.
- Cut facings from lining fabric rather than heavy pile fabrics or those with beads and sequins.
- Change needles and pins frequently, particularly when sewing fabrics with metallic fibers which can blunt them easily.
- When working with flimsy fabrics, use lots of pins in the seam allowance to keep the layers together.
- When working with faux leather and suede, use weights or tin cans rather than pins which will leave holes.

- Stitch all seams in the direction of the nap whenever possible.
- Use sew-in interfacings.
- Follow the "with nap" layout to ensure any shading, pile, or pattern runs in the same direction.
- Always use a press cloth and press with care. Avoid pressing fabrics that have pre-pressed surface detail such as crushed velvets or pre-pleated fabric.

Checked and striped fabric

- Only use striped or checked fabrics with patterns that list them in the suggested fabrics.

- Make sure the fabric design matches across the garment by placing the paper pattern on a single layer of fabric. Turn the pattern piece over to cut the corresponding section, to get a left and a right piece.
- Make sure the balance marks and notches are in line across all the matching pattern pieces.
- When placing a pattern on fabric, ensure the most dominant stripe or check is not placed at the widest body point, such as the bust or hips. Match checks and stripes at the same point on the pattern pieces. Discount seam allowances when matching patterns.
- It is not possible for checks and stripes to match at all seams, so choose the most prominent places for pattern matching.

Beaded, sequinned fabrics
- Use a zipper foot to stitch beaded fabrics if the beading prevents straight stitching. Use a walking foot to sew heavy-pile fabric to help the layers feed evenly.
- To eliminate bulk in the seams, remove beading from the seam allowance by crushing the beads (use a little hammer or two spoons) and gently removing. Cut sequins in half and pull out.
- Avoid steam when working with beaded, sequin, or metallic fabrics.

Fabrics with pile
- Trim the pile from the seam allowance to reduce bulk. To hide seams in furs, working from the right side, use a pin to pick out the pile from the seam stitching.
- When pressing fabrics with a pile or heavy texture, use a soft towel as a pressing surface or velvet board.

Sheer, fancy fabrics

- On transparent, sheer, and lacy fabrics, use French seams, or double-stitched or rolled hems, which look good on both sides of the fabric. Alternatively, bind seams and hems with a fine bias tape or lace edging.
- Use a small hole throat plate when sewing very fine fabrics to prevent the fabric being pulled into the throat plate.

Stretch fabrics

- For close-fitting knit garments, cut the pattern pieces slightly smaller than the actual size.
- Use zigzag or stretch stitches to sew knit fabrics.
- To prevent knit fabric edges curling, stitch a double row of stitching and trim close to the outer row.
- Stay stitch or stay tape any areas that are not supposed to stretch, such as the neck, armhole, and shoulder seams.

FABRIC REQUIREMENTS

To determine the amount of fabric required when the fabric width of your chosen fabric differs from the pattern guidelines, use the chart below. Note that one-way designs, checks, and stripes may need more fabric than the recommended amount.

For example, if a pattern calls for 1¾ yd (1.60 m) of 45 in (115 cm)-wide fabric, and your chosen fabric is 36 in (90 cm) wide, go to the 45 in (115 cm) column, look down until you get to 1¾ yd (1.60 m) and then move along the row until you get to the 36 in (90 cm) column. The amount of fabric required at the different width will be noted in this column, i.e. 2¼ yd (2.10 m).

FABRIC WIDTHS							
90 cm meter	36 in yard	115 cm meter	45 in yard	140 cm meter	54 in yard	150 cm meter	60 in yard
1.60	1¾	1.30	1⅜	1.05	1⅛	0.95	1
1.85	2	1.50	1⅝	1.30	1⅜	1.15	1¼
2.10	2¼	1.60	1¾	1.50	1½	1.30	1⅜
2.30	2½	1.95	2⅛	1.60	1¾	1.50	1⅝
2.65	2⅞	2.10	2¼	1.75	1⅞	1.60	1¾
2.90	3⅛	2.30	2½	1.85	2	1.75	1⅞
3.10	3⅜	2.55	2¾	2.10	2¼	1.85	2
3.45	3¾	2.65	2⅞	2.20	2⅜	2.10	2¼
3.90	4¼	2.90	3⅛	2.40	2⅝	2.20	2⅜
4.15	4½	3.10	3⅜	2.55	2¾	2.40	2⅝
4.35	4¾	3.35	3⅝	2.65	2⅞	2.55	2¾
4.60	5	3.55	3⅞	2.90	3⅛	2.65	2⅞

THREADS AND NOTIONS

The choice of threads, notions, and cutting equipment available today means there is a tool for every task, many of which also make the job easier.

THREADS

As well as all-purpose sewing threads, there are a number of specialty threads and natural fiber threads, all of which are available in a wide range of colors.

All-purpose threads – Today most all-purpose threads are polyester-coated cottons which have the flexibility of polyester with the strength of cotton. This type of thread is perfectly acceptable for most general sewing projects. You will also find 100% polyester threads, which are stronger.

Silk threads – These are very soft and have a sheen, making them ideal for hand sewing or top stitching.

Machine embroidery – These are slightly finer than all-purpose threads because they are often used in highly concentrated stitch patterns. Most have a high gloss. They are often 100% polyester or rayon. There is a huge variety of threads, ranging from plain, vibrant colors to metallics, variegated and iridescent. Use with a machine embroidery needle that has a larger eye suitable

All-purpose threads

for highly dense stitching, which will also help prevent the thread splitting or breaking.

Bobbin fill – Designed for use with machine embroidery, this is a finer black or white thread used in the bobbin, and thus forming the underside of heavily stitched embroideries. Because it is finer, it decreases the density of the stitching on the reverse of the work, which helps prevent puckering.

Metallic threads – Used for decorative stitching either by hand or machine. If machining, use with a metallic needle which has a coated eye because

Embroidery threads

Metallic threads

the metallic fibers can cut a minute groove in the eye, causing threads to shred and snap. Use thicker, uneven metallic threads on the bobbin rather than as the upper thread. Sew with the work facing downward to ensure the decorative thread is on the right side.

Top stitch/buttonhole thread – Designed to be highly visible, this is a thicker thread, most often polyester. It is used for top stitching, decorative stitches, or hand sewing buttons, etc. Use an all-purpose thread in the bobbin and a jeans needle or machine embroidery needle with a larger eye to accommodate the thicker thread.

Quilting thread – This thread has a wax finish to help prevent tangling when hand stitching. A poly cotton blend or 100% cotton, it can also be used for machine stitching.

Basting thread – Usually 100% cotton, basting thread is finer and rougher than general thread. It will break easily and is only used for temporarily holding fabrics together.

Invisible/transparent thread – Available in clear or smoke color, it is a nylon thread designed for attaching trims, quilting, and repairs.

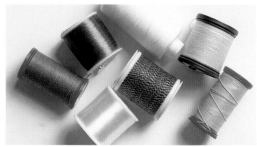

Speciality threads

HAND-SEWING THREADS

In addition to the machine threads which can be used for hand sewing, there are different, thicker threads used for embroidery, cross stitch, crochet, crewel, and stumpwork. They are available in an extensive range of colors and varieties, on skeins, braids, or spools and may be a mix of fibers or 100% cotton.

Mercerized or Perlé crochet thread – Used for cross stitch or crochet, it is usually 100% cotton and has a slight luster.

Embroidery floss/stranded cotton – As the name suggests, these are made up of strands which can be separated and used separately or in combinations of 1–6, depending on the thickness required, to form stitches. Varieties include high sheen, matte finish, variegated in silks, cotton, linen, or mixed fibers.

HELPFUL HINT:
When choosing thread, hold a piece of fabric against the spool. If a perfect match isn't possible, choose a slightly darker shade as it will look lighter when unravelled off the spool.

Embroidery flosses

Serger cones

SERGING THREADS

As sergers (overlockers) use far more thread than a conventional sewing machine, specially designed threads come on larger cones, cops, and spools (also known as bobbins). There are different qualities, each used for slightly different finishes. However, sewing machine decorative threads can be used in the loopers (which have larger-eyed needles).

100% spun polyester/cotton wrapped polyester – Used in the needles, these threads are similar to sewing machine threads but finer.

Woolly nylon/floss – As the name suggests, this has a flossy/woolly texture with a slight sheen. It is used in the upper looper so that the soft wool is on the upper edge of the seam and is ideal for swimwear, fabrics with Lycra, and lingerie. Bulk thread is similar without the sheen. It is good for stretch and knit fabrics.

Decorative threads – Conventional decorative threads can be used in the loopers which have larger-eyed needles.

CUTTING TOOLS

There are all types of scissors, designed to make the cutting task easier. A good, basic selection will include dressmaking shears, pinking shears, embroidery scissors, all-purpose scissors, and a scissor sharpener.

Shears –These have molded handles, with a smaller hole for the thumb and a larger one for the fingers. They are shaped for right- or left-hand use. Blades are long and straight for smooth, long cuts. Handles may be angled from the blades so the blades sit parallel with the cutting surface and fabric remains flat. Some dressmaking shears have very fine serrated blades on the cutting edge which grip slippery fabric while cutting.

Pinking shears – As with dressmaking shears, these have shaped handles. The blades have a pronounced zigzag cutting edge that "pink" fabrics to finish raw edges. Use for finishing cottons, craft fabrics, and other non-fray fabrics.

All-purpose scissors – Similar to shears, but the scissor handles have the same size apertures for fingers and thumb and can be used right- or left-handed. Some shears and scissors have soft touch handles, and a spongy surface within the grip area

Shears and all-purpose scissors

that makes handling and prolonged cutting easier on the hand. Spring-touch scissors have handles one on top of the other and are designed for single hand use.

Needlework/embroidery scissors – Small scissors are convenient for snipping and clipping into tight curves and around notches, etc. Those with curved tips are particularly useful for snipping threads close to machine embroidery work.

Embroidery scissors

Seam ripper and scissor sharpener

Sharpeners – Designed to remove burrs and nicks in scissor blades, these handy gadgets also keep scissors sharp for longer. However, they cannot be used with serrated blade or pinking shears.

Seam ripper – Also known as a quick-unpick, this is a useful tool for removing unwanted stitches quickly. Simply slip the blade under the stitch and slice through, repeating every 1–2 in (2.5–5 cm).

HELPFUL HINT:
Use a seam ripper to open buttonholes neatly – push a pin through the fabric at one end, and slice with the ripper from the other end, working toward the pin.

Rotary cutters – Used in conjunction with a ruler and self-healing cutting mat, rotary cutters are used to cut long, straight lengths of fabric quickly and easily. Some cutters have retractable blades or blades with different cutting edges. They are usually very sharp so care should be taken when using them. They are ideal for patchwork and quilting, cutting bias strips and fabric for soft furnishings.

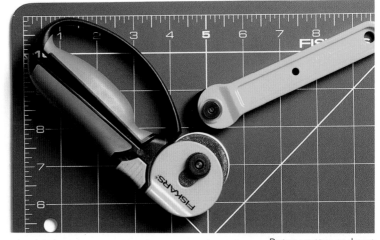

Rotary cutter and mat

MARKING TOOLS

A number of different types of marking tool are available, used to transfer pattern-matching notes from the tissue pattern to the fabric. Whenever possible, mark the reverse of the fabric.

Chalk – Easily removed after use, chalk markers are quick and easy to use. Available in a variety of shapes and colors, there are chalk wheels, chalk pencils, and chalk blocks. Chalk wheels work in one direction only and leave a fine trail of powder. Blocks can be used in any direction and leave a heavier line, while chalk pencils are used in the same way as ordinary pencils.

Marker pens – Some of the different types available include water-soluble, fadeaway, and permanent. They are used in the same way as a normal pen. Vanishing or fadeaway pens and pencils are also known as evaporating or air-soluble pens. Marks simply fade away after about 48 hours. Water-soluble pens are usually blue. The mark can be removed later by sponging or washing.

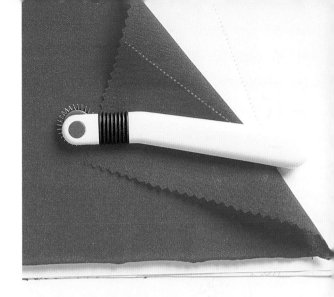

Carbon paper and tracing wheel

Dressmaker's carbon paper and tracing wheel – A traditional marking tool, carbon papers are now available in a range of colors. There are also vanishing carbons. They can be used to mark two fabric layers at the same time by placing a folded sheet between fabric layers. As with all markings, use on the reverse of the fabric.

Chalk markers and marker pens

HELPFUL HINT:
To mark darts, snip a hole in the tissue at the dart placement mark and use chalk to mark the spot. Pin through the fabric layers at this spot and, turning the layers over, make a chalk mark on the underside at the same point.

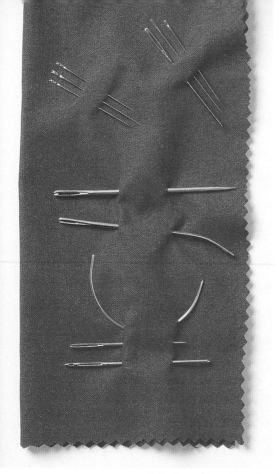

Selection of hand needles

NEEDLES

There is a huge variety of needles for both hand and machine sewing, with a selection of all-purpose needles and those designed for very specific jobs. Following is a list of the most common needles.

Hand needles

The length, point type, size of eye, and shape of needle depends on the task for which it is designed. For instance, tapestry needles have blunt points, and upholstery needles are curved so that they can be inserted and come out on the same side (essential when you can't get to the back of the work).

Mixed hand needles – Essential in every household, mixed hand needles provide a selection of different length and eye-size needles to cope with general sewing repairs.

Ballpoint needles – Used when sewing knit and stretch fabrics, these have a rounded point which parts rather than pierces the fabric fibers.

Beading needles – These are used for adding beads by hand and are often curved. They are very fine with a small, flat eye to go through small beads easily.

Self-threading needles – Fairly new on the market and ideal for partially sighted people, a split eye at the top makes threading a breeze.

Darning needles – These have a fairly blunt point and large eye to cope with heavier threads.

Upholstery needles – Some are curved, as mentioned above, and others have extra large eyes to take very thick threads or are extra long.

Bodkins – Used for threading elastic or ribbons through casings, a bodkin is not really a needle, but is shaped like one, with a rounded point and large, flat eye.

HELPFUL HINT:
Replace needles frequently because they will blunt over time and can snag delicate or knit fabrics, thereby spoiling the look of your work. For easy threading, cut thread at an angle.

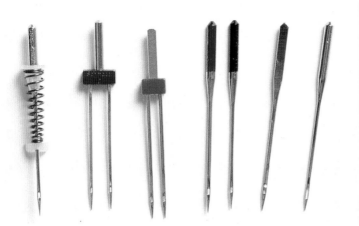

Selection of machine needles

Machine needles

As with hand needles, there are different machine needles for different types of fabric and techniques. Using the right needle will help ensure even, neat stitches.

One side of the needle shaft is flattened to ensure correct insertion into the needle aperture. Generally it is flat to back, but check your user's manual. Incorrect insertion can cause skipped stitches. Always tighten the needle in position using the screwdriver supplied in your sewing machine's tool kit, otherwise it can work loose or move about when stitching.

HELPFUL HINT:
For every new project, use a fresh needle. If using special needles for small amounts of sewing, paint the shaft with nail polish to color-code them.

HELPFUL HINT:
If a seam pulls up or stitches are skipped, the needle may be too big; try a smaller size. If it breaks when stitching, it may be too small; try a larger size.

NEEDLE SIZES
American sizes range from 9 to 20, while European sizes go from 60 to 120. Packs are usually numbered with both American and European sizing.
Use the following as a guide:
9–11 (60–75) For lightweight fabrics such as chiffon, voiles, organza, silks, and lingerie
12–14 (80–90) For medium-weight fabrics and general dressmaking fabrics such as cottons, woolens, and polyesters
16–18 (100–110) For heavyweight fabrics and coatings such as heavy brocade, dense denim, and canvas
20 (120) For very heavyweight, thick, and coarse fabrics

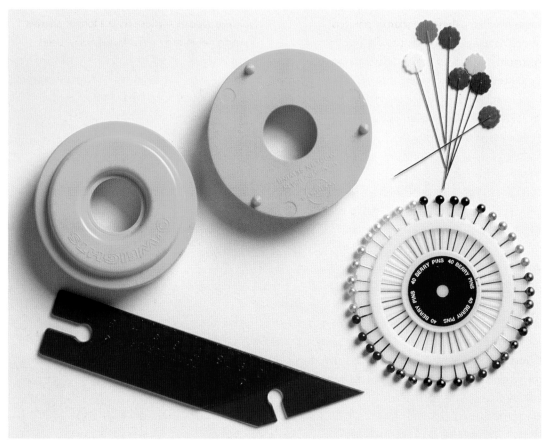

Weights, dressmaking pins, and a point turner

Common needle types

All-purpose, universal needles – Used for general sewing projects, they have a sharp point and come in different sizes to suit different fabric weights.

Sharps/microfiber needles – These have sharp points and are used for densely woven fabrics. Used for silks, buttonholes, top stitching.

Ballpoint needles – As with hand ballpoint needles, they have rounded tips to part the fibers as they stitch. Used for stretch knits, jerseys, fleece, and velvet.

Embroidery/machine embroidery needles – These have a larger eye to cope with embroidery threads and novelty threads. Used with machine embroidery threads and for top stitching.

Metallic thread needles – Like embroidery needles, these have a larger eye, usually specially coated for extra protection against metallic threads that can wear away a small nick in the eye, causing the threads to break and shred. Used for metallic threads and machine embroidery.

Twin needles – Used to stitch two parallel rows of stitching at the same time, they have two needles on one shaft. Twin needles are available in universal, embroidery, stretch, and ballpoint varieties. The distance between the needles can vary from 1/16–1/8 in (2–3 mm). Used for decorative top stitching and heirloom stitching.

Jeans needles – These are sharply pointed strong needles, often with a blue top for easy recognition. Used for denim, heavy canvas, upholstery fabric, faux suede, and top stitching.

Leather needles – To help penetrate leather, these needles have a triangular chisel point. Note: any stitches made will leave little holes so always test before stitching the main project. Used for leather, suede, and faux suede.

Stretch needles – Designed with a "scarf" to help pierce two-way stretch fabric. Used for swimwear, Lycra, rubber, and lingerie.

Wing needles – These have a larger-shaped eye and are designed to leave little holes in the fabric as they stitch. Used for heirloom stitching.

Quilting needles – These have a longer, sharper point to penetrate several layers easily. Used for quilting.

Spring needles – These quite literally have a spring wrapped around the needle shaft. They can be used without a presser foot. Used for free-motion embroidery.

Sergers (overlockers)

A variety of needles are also available for sergers, some of which are interchangeable with sewing machine needles. Check your user's manual.

PINS AND WEIGHTS

Pins are like needles and can blunt with repeated use. Change them regularly to prevent fabrics being snagged or laddered. Use weights (or tin cans) instead of pins when cutting out leather or fabrics that can be damaged by pin marks. Weights are also ideal when working on a large, flat surface.

As with needles, there are a number of different types of pins to suit different fabrics and tasks. These range from sharp, universal, ballpoint, quilting, lace, and upholstery pins. Dressmaking pins are usually made from tempered, hardened steel. Some varieties have glass or plastic ball or flower heads which make removing and finding them easier. Take care when pressing: the plastic head can melt under a hot iron!

Use pin basting instead of thread basting for quick and easy projects. Pin every 2–3 in (5–8 cm) on fine, slippery fabrics; every 3–4 in (8–10 cm) on light- to medium-weight fabrics, and 5–6 in (13–15 cm) on heavyweight fabrics. Increase the number of pins at curves and when fitting two sections together such as sleeves into armholes or a skirt onto a waistband.

HELPFUL HINTS:
* Pin tissue to the fabric in the seam allowances, with pins parallel to the cutting line.
* When pin basting, always position the pins so they are at right angles to the work so the pins can be removed as you stitch.

Seam roll and tailor's ham

HANDY ACCESSORIES

As well as all the scissors, pins and needles, and marking tools, there are a few other sewing aids that make life a little easier.

Point turner – Shaped to an angled point at one end, this useful tool also has measurements along one side. Used to push corners out fully on collars, cushion corners, etc. They are also used for measuring hem allowances.

Rouleau turner – Long, thin, and with a hook at one end, this device is used to turn fine tubing through to the right side.

PRESSING TOOLS

To achieve a professional finish to sewing projects, pressing accurately and often is essential. As well as a steam iron and press cloth, other useful pressing tools include the following:

Sleeve board – As the name suggests, this is a miniature ironing board used for ironing sleeves.

Seam roll – A well-stuffed, sausage-shaped cloth roll, it is used to press over long, straight seams without the underside being pressed at the same time – such as sleeves, shoulder yokes. A tightly rolled towel works just as well.

Tailor's ham – This is a stuffed, ham-shaped oval, hence the name. Use it to press open curved areas such as darts and princess seams.

Velvet/needle board – Used to press fabrics with a pile such as velvets, corduroy, and fleece, it is a pad covered with fine steel needles. A soft, fluffy towel works well as an alternative.

Pressing techniques

Pressing differs from ironing in that the iron is not moved back and forth, rather it is placed on the work, held for a moment, lifted, and moved to the next position. This avoids fabrics being stretched as they are pressed.

- Press each seam as it is sewn and before being stitched over again.
- Press from the wrong side whenever possible using a press cloth.
- Before applying steam, test a fabric sample to see how it reacts.
- Leave work to cool fully before continuing.

HELPFUL HINT:
Use a transparent fabric, such as organza, as a press cloth so you can see what is being pressed through the cloth.

INTERFACINGS AND STABILIZERS

Interfacings are used to enhance the look of a garment, adding firmness and stability to specific areas such as collars, cuffs, and front facings. Stabilizers are used to back fabric, holding it taut while stitching, particularly when doing machine embroidery.

Selection of interfacings

INTERFACINGS

There are many different types of interfacing, ranging from soft, pliable ones to heavier, stiff canvas types for soft furnishings. Which to use depends on personal preference, the fabric being interfaced, and the desired finish.

Generally, lightweight interfacings are used with lightweight fabrics. For very lightweight, transparent fabrics, an extra layer of the main fabric is sometimes used.

There are three main categories of interfacing, all of which come in fusible (iron-on) and sew-in varieties, in white, black, and nude colors, and in different weights.

Nonwoven — Made from pressed fibers with a felt-like appearance. Because there is no grain, they can be cut in any direction and pattern pieces placed any way up. Weights range from super light to extra heavy. Used for traditional home dressmaking and crafts.

Woven — These have a grain and are cut on the grain or bias in the same way as fabrics are. The super lightweights are ideal for silks, georgettes, sheers, and satins. Medium- to heavyweight interfacings are used for jackets, dresses, and blouses.

Knitted — These are made with a two-way stretch so they handle like knitted fabrics. Used for sportswear, knitted, stretch, and pile fabrics.

SPECIALTY INTERFACINGS

In addition to interfacings for general use, there are specialty versions for different sewing techniques including waistbanding, hemming, stay tape, craft, and soft furnishing interfacings.

Waistbandings – Designed to be used in waistbands, front bands, and pleats, they are nonwoven and are usually fusible. Some have slotted lines to help fold and sew easily. Others have stiffened bands attached to the interfacing to provide roll-resistance in waistbands.

Hem tapes – Again, usually fusible, these are used to turn up hems without stitching. Hem web is a double-sided, very fine adhesive strip that melts, bonding the fabric when pressed. It is placed between the hem allowance and the main fabric. Bondahem is similar but has a paper backing so it can be applied in two stages or used to attach pockets, etc. Blind hem tape is folded to mimic a sewn blind hem. Usually fusible, it is applied in the same way as hem webbing.

Bias tape – This is used to prevent unwanted stretch at necklines, armhole edges, or any curve that needs stabilizing. It is a bias-cut fusible tape and is used within the seam allowance.

Stay tape – As with the bias tape, stay tape is used to add stability in areas that you don't want to stretch too much. It is a straight cut, narrow

Selection of hem tapes

strip with reinforced stitching for added hold. It is very useful for adding firmness to areas which have been cut on the bias, such as shoulder seams and skirt slits.

Fleece, wadding, or batting – This describes the soft interfacings that are used to add padding, bulk, and warmth to quilts and other soft furnishings. Specialty versions include those made of compressed fleece which provides some heat resistance or those with preprinted guidelines for quilting. Waddings and battings are described as having extra loft – otherwise known as bulk density.

Batting comes in a variety of different weights, from lightweight (2 oz), to more heavyweight (12 oz). If you are making an item for a baby, such as a crib bumper, make sure that the batting you are using conforms to safety standards.

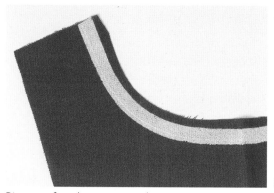

Bias tape fused onto a curved area

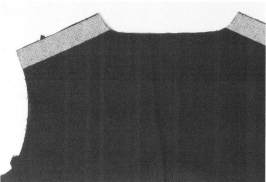

Stay tape applied to a shoulder edge

APPLYING INTERFACINGS

Sew-in – Use sew-in on textured fabrics, those with pile, beading, and sequins. Stitch the interfacing to the wrong side of the fabric piece just within the seam allowance and then trim close to the stitching so that there is none in the seam allowance. Trim the corners at an angle.

Iron-on (fusible) interfacing – Although very quick and easy to apply, iron-on interfacings and tapes must be fused properly to ensure they remain fixed, even when laundered. To apply, cut fusible interfacing to the size of the pattern piece then trim so it fits within the seam allowance. Fuse to the wrong side of the fabric, using a press cloth and dry iron. Press for approximately 10–15 seconds before lifting the iron and repositioning (do not slide the iron along as it might push the interfacing out of position). The actual time taken to fuse completely will differ between fabric and interfacing weights. Always test on a sample first. Allow to cool completely before continuing to work with the fabric.

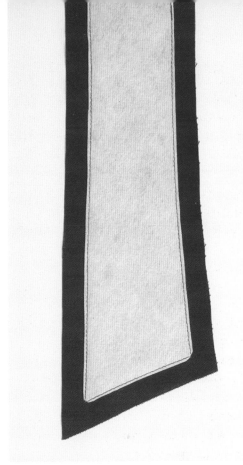

Sew-in interfacing

Iron-on (fusible) interfacing

Selection of stabilizers

STABILIZERS

A stabilizer is used to back areas that are to be densely stitched, such as machine embroidery, buttonholes, and appliqué. Varieties include tearaway, water-soluble, heat-off, self-adhesive, and permanent stabilizers. Stabilizers help prevent fine fabrics being pulled down into the throat plate and the fabric puckering when stitched.

Tearaway – Crisp to handle with a flat, felt-like finish, tearaway stabilizers are positioned on the reverse of the fabric, under the area to be stitched. After stitching, simply tear away the excess.

Water-soluble – There are many types of water-soluble stabilizer, ranging from very fine, fabric-like qualities to heavy-duty films. They are used in areas that need stabilizing while being stitched, but which need to be removed afterward. They can also be used on the front of work to prevent stitches disappearing into pile fabrics such as velvet and towelling. Use them in single

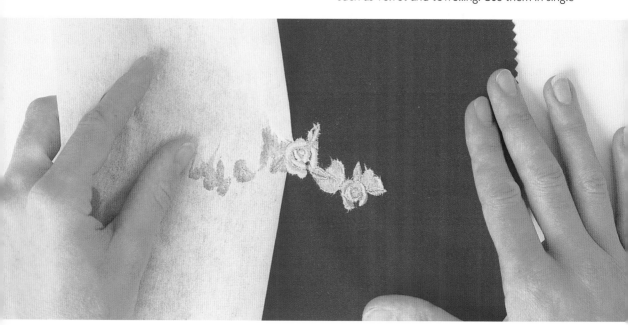

Take care when pulling away a tearaway stabilizer because you do not want to spoil your work.

HELPFUL HINT:
To create stitched sculptures, use the heavy-duty soluble stabilizer and wash gently until the desired crispness remains.

Paper-backed fusible web

or multiple layers, depending on the thickness of the pile. Very fine fabrics should be sandwiched between two layers of stabilizer.

Once the area has been stitched, wash away the stabilizer by soaking the work in cold water. The stabilizer will just dissolve away. Rinse well. Heat-off versions are removed by ironing the area—the stabilizer turns brown then crumbles away.

Water-soluble stabilizer

Self-adhesive embroidery backer – This is used to back small areas such as cap peaks, cuffs, and collars. It has a layer of paper covering the adhesive side. Once hooped, the garment section can be adhered to the embroidery backer by removing the paper from the appropriate area.

Paper-backed fusible web – This is a double-sided fusible web, backed on one side with paper. It is ideal for applying appliqué. The designs to be appliquéd are drawn on the paper backing (in reverse) then cut out roughly. Position this on the wrong side of the fabric, web side to fabric, and fuse in place. Cut out accurately and then place in position, peeling the paper backing away. Again, press in place. Finish with satin stitch or zigzag stitch to seal the edges. Alternatively, use fabric paint.

PAPER PATTERNS

Paper patterns are readily available for all kinds of sewing, from dressmaking to crafts and soft furnishings. The majority of the commercial pattern brands use the same sizing code, pattern markings, and terminology.

THE PATTERN PACK

Inside commercial patterns there are tissue sheets on which are printed all the full-size paper pattern pieces plus illustrated step-by-step construction notes. On the envelope itself are photographs or illustrations of the garments or projects included in the pack, line drawings showing details such as zippers, buttons, and darts, a list and quantity guide for all materials and notions required, suggested fabrics, and a table of sizes and measurements.

Pattern sizing – Shown on the envelope are the main measurements – bust, waist, hip, back length. Check these against your own personal measurements to determine your pattern size

Note: it may not be the same as your ready-to-wear size. If you are different sizing for top and bottoms, use your hip measurement for trousers and skirts and your bust measurement for tops, jackets, and dresses.

Garment sizes – These may be listed on the envelope or on the tissue pieces. They will give the measurements of the finished garment, which will include wearing ease and designer ease and thus can be considerably bigger than your personal body measurements.

Suggested fabrics – This section includes a list of suitable fabrics. Although other fabrics can be used, only those recommended have been tested. In particular, avoid using checks and stripes unless listed.

Fabric requirements – Noted on the reverse of the envelope, the list includes requirements for different fabric widths and sizes. It will also include "with nap" and "without nap" requirements. Follow with-nap quantities when working with pile, novelty, or fabrics with sheen.

Tissue pattern – Many dressmaking patterns are multi-size and thus have cutting lines for each size around each piece. There may also be a choice of notch and dart positions. Follow the lines that correspond to your size. Most international patterns include seam allowances within the pattern pieces, which are generally ⅝ in (1.5 cm).

SIZING

In commercial patterns an average woman is categorized as "Misses," and is 5 ft 5 in–5 ft 6 in (165–168 cm) tall with a B cup size (see the measurements charts on pages 54–55). Women or Women Plus patterns are for those with fuller figures while teen designs are categorized as Junior/Teen, and children's patterns are sized by age and average measurements.

The wearing ease, mentioned earlier, is the amount of "wriggle" room that has been incorporated. Therefore a coat that is designed to wear over a jacket will have ample room, while a boned bodice will have very little. In addition, there might be "designer" ease, built in by the designer to create the style envisaged.

PATTERN TERMINOLOGY

In addition to sizing, the terminology used by pattern companies is fairly universal. Pattern instructions and pattern pieces have various markings to help with fitting together, lengthening, shortening, and shaping.

1. *Pattern number, section, number of pieces to be cut.*
2. *Notches* – matched evenly side to side, back to front, etc. Cut notches outward into fabric.
3. *Multi-size cutting lines* – follow the line for your size. When lines converge, follow the single line.
4. *Circles* – used as placement marks for pockets, etc., or to indicate where to stop and start stitching. Transfer to the fabric with a marking pen, chalk, or tailor's tacks (see hand stitching, page 58).
5. *Lengthen/shorten line* – adjust length at this point. Fold pattern up to shorten by the required amount, or cut through the tissue and separate by the required amount to lengthen.
6. *Darts* – transfer the markings from the tissue to the fabric. Darts are used to shape garments. On multi-size patterns, follow the darts for your size only.
7. *Grain line* – this line should run perfectly parallel with the selvage. Measure from the line to the selvage at either end to ensure it is accurate.
8. *Fold line* – place the pattern piece on the fold of the fabric so that when cut out the piece is double the size and symmetrical. Fold the fabric right sides together, with the selvages parallel.
9. *Pleats, tucks, and buttonholes* – these lines indicate where to take or make pleats, tucks, and buttonholes. Transfer to the fabric as with circles and darts.

Pattern piece with markings

Other sewing terminology, used frequently in construction notes, includes the following:

Selvage – The bound side edges of the fabric.

Grain – The direction of the weave on woven fabrics. The lengthwise or straight grain runs parallel with the selvages. The crosswise grain runs from selvage to selvage and the bias is a diagonal; true bias is at a 45-degree angle from the lengthwise grain.

Nap – Indicates a fabric with a pile, sheen, or textural surface that goes one way. All pieces cut from nap fabric must be cut facing the same way to prevent uneven shading. Use "with nap" layouts for checks, plaids, and any patterned fabric with a one-way design. If possible, use with the nap running downward. With-nap layouts usually require more fabric than those without.

Notching and clipping – These terms describe how to treat curved seams to ensure they lay flat. Notching is cutting wedge-shaped triangles from the seam allowance on outer curves. Clip into the seam allowance of inner curves, cutting close to stitching every 1½ in (2.5–3 cm) (diagram 1).

Grading seams – Used to reduce the bulk of fabric within the seams on heavier fabrics. The two seam allowances of each layer of fabric are cut a different width. Cut the under seam allowance to a minimal ⅛ in (3 mm) and the top seam allowance that will lie closest to the outer fabric ¼ in (6 mm) (diagram 2).

Diagram 1: Notching and clipping

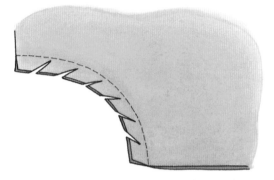

Diagram 2: Grading seams

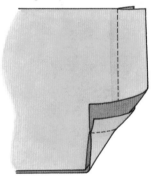

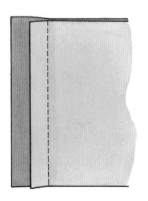

FABRIC LAYOUTS

Fabric layouts showing how to place pattern pieces on fabric are provided for each of the views included in the pattern. There will be layouts for different fabric widths, with and without nap. All the pattern pieces needed for each view are also noted next to the layout which also shows whether to cut pieces from single or double layers of fabric (diagram 3).

Diagram 3: Fabric layouts

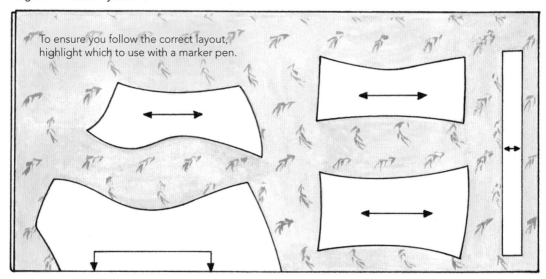

To ensure you follow the correct layout, highlight which to use with a marker pen.

PATTERN ALTERATIONS

Today most commercial patterns are multi-sized with three or more sizes printed on the tissue paper for each piece. The sizes differ at crucial fitting points, such as neck, bust, waist, hip, and crotch as well as being slightly smaller or bigger in width, while at other areas, the size lines converge. Unfortunately it is not a matter of simply increasing a pattern piece by the same amount all around. Pattern alterations are also needed to suit individual figure varations such as for a larger, fuller bust, fuller upper arms, higher or lower bottom, wider hips, or a thicker waist.

The following are basic alterations only. Check the fit by tissue fitting or making a sample garment in muslin before cutting out fashion fabrics. Remember to alter all corresponding pattern pieces, i.e., front, back, and facings.

Lengthening or shortening – For minimal differences, adjust at the hemline. However, for more than 1¼ in (3 cm), use the lengthen/shorten line on the pattern tissue, which is placed to ensure the style isn't spoiled when the garment length is altered. On patterns without lengthen lines:

- *Back neck to waist length* – alter midway between the bust and the waist. Redraw any darts that are affected.
- *Waist to hem* – alter between the hip and the hem (if not altering at hemline).
- *A-line dress and skirt* – alter below the hipline.
- *Sleeves* – alter partway down the sleeve.
- *Trousers/shorts* – to increase/decrease the crotch depth, alter below the darts but above the crotchline.

To lengthen, cut the pattern piece across the width and spread apart by the desired amount. Add extra tissue in the gap and tape together. Redraw any darts or princess seaming. To shorten,

Diagram 4: Lengthening or shortening

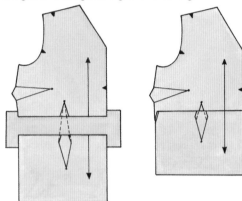

fold tissue paper across the width by the desired amount. Tape in position. Again redraw darts if necessary (diagram 4).

Darts – Used to add shape to flat fabric, these can be increased in size, decreased, added, or left out completely in order to shape more or less of the fabric to fit over fuller busts, rounded or flat bottoms, etc. For example, people with flat bottoms require thin short darts and

All darts should be pressed over a ham or curve to create the shape in the fabric.

Diagram 5: Bust darts

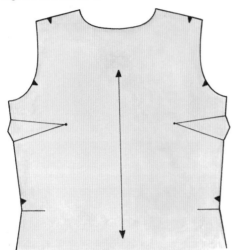

Diagram 6: Waist darts

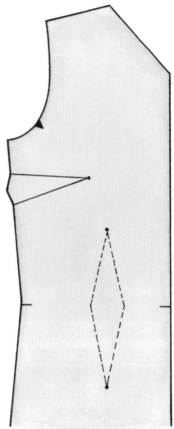

minimal shaping, while those with fuller bottoms require deeper, curved darts. The same applies for tummies.

- Bust darts should apex just before the fullest point of the bust. Pin out the dart on the tissue paper and check the position against your body—if it is not in the right place, mark your apex on the tissue then redraw the dart stitching lines from the new point to the original base at the seam line (diagram 5).

- Waist darts are used to shape and fit fabric through the torso. These can be increased or decreased to take in more or less fabric. Waist darts also need shortening if bust darts are lowered so that darts are not too close. Simply shorten the waist darts so the distance between the apex of the bust and the top of the waist dart remains the same as before the alterations (diagram 6).

GENERAL TIPS

- Always pre-wash and press the fabric before cutting, particularly when adding linings (which might otherwise shrink at different levels).
- Seam allowances are usually included in patterns; look for them in the instructions and note when they vary.
- Cut out around the notches and transfer all other pattern markings to the fabric.
- Fold the fabric right sides together unless otherwise stated, folded lengthwise with selvages together. When the pattern is cut on folded fabric, there will be a right and left piece cut at the same time.
- When cutting a bias-cut garment, work with a single layer of fabric. Remember, to get a right- and left-hand section, it is then necessary to flip the pattern over.
- Place the pattern on the fabric right side up unless otherwise stated.

- Place all pattern pieces with the straight of grain line in the same direction, i.e., top to bottom.
- The grain line on the pattern tissue (straight line in center of tissue piece) should run parallel to the selvage.
- To increase or decrease a pattern size, the difference between tissue size and own measurements has to be divided by the number of pieces. Therefore if there are two front pieces and two back pieces, divide the difference by 4 so that a little is added to each piece at the side seam.
- Cut out and make up a muslin sample if you are unsure of the sizing – this will avoid costly mistakes.
- Use notches to match side seams, etc. Use circular or triangular points to match placement for pockets and folds for darts and pleats.
- Read all pattern instructions before starting.

MEASURING GUIDE

Before deciding which commercial pattern size you need to make, it is first necessary to take some basic body measurements. Wear your usual underwear and, standing barefoot, take bust, waist, hip, high bust, and back neck to waist measurements.

BASIC BODY MEASUREMENTS

Bust – Measure around the fullest part of the bust and straight across the back. The tape should remain parallel to the floor.

High bust – This is directly under the arms and above the bust and straight across the back.

Waist – To find the natural waistline tie a string around the waist and bend side to side. It will roll into the crease that forms at the natural waistline.

Hips – Measure at the fullest part – approximately 7–9 in (18–23 cm) below waist (diagram 1).

Diagram 1: Basic body measurements

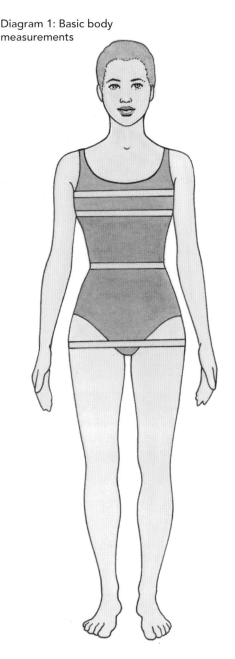

HELPFUL HINTS:
* If you are making skirts, trousers, and shorts, use the hip measurement to determine the pattern size.
* If you are making jackets, tops, and dresses, use the bust measurement to determine the pattern size.
* If the difference between the bust and the high bust measurement is more than 2½ in (6.5 cm), select the pattern size by the high bust measurement.

Diagram 2:
Back waist length

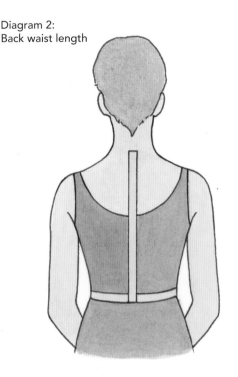

Diagram 3:
Crotch depth

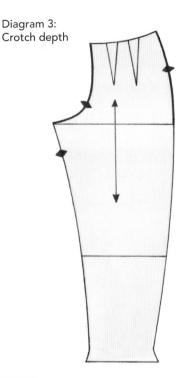

OTHER USEFUL MEASUREMENTS

Back waist length – From the base of the neck (most prominent bone) to the natural waistline (diagram 2).

Bust point – Measure from the base of the neck/ shoulder to the fullest point of the bust. On a paper pattern check this measurement (remember to allow for seam allowances), it should be 1 in (2.5 cm) from the dart point.

Shoulder length – From the base of the neck to the shoulder edge. If it is broader or narrower than the pattern piece, adjustments to the pattern will need to be made.

Crotch length – Measure from the waistline at the back, down through the legs to the waistline at the front. Divide the measurement into front and back crotch lengths at the mid-point between the legs. Check the measurements against the tissue pattern crotch line. If the pattern needs to be altered, make alterations below the dart and above the crotch.

Crotch depth – Sit on a hard chair to take the measurement from the waistline to the seat down the outside leg seam line. Check the measurement against the pattern as above (diagram 3).

Imperial

Misses'/Miss Petite – For well-proportioned, developed figures.

Misses' about 5' 5" to 5' 6" without shoes. Miss Petite under 5' 4" without shoes.

Sizes	4/ US 2	6/ US 4	8/ US 6	10/ US 8	12/ US 10	14/ US 12	16/ US 14	18/ US 16	20/ US 18	22/ US 20	24/ US 22	26/ US 24	
Sizes – European	30	32	34	36	38	40	42	44	46	48	50	52	
Bust	29½	30½	31½	32½	34	36	38	40	42	44	46	48	in
Waist	22	23	24	25	26½	28	30	32	34	37	38	41½	in
Hip – 9 in below waist	31½	32½	33½	34½	36	38	40	42	44	46	48	50	in
Back waist length	15½	15½	15¾	16	16¼	16½	16¾	17	17¼	17⅜	17½	17¾	in
Petite – back waist length	14¼	14½	14¾	15	15¼	15½	15¾	16	16¼	16⅜	16½	16⅝	in

Women's/Women's Petite – For the larger, more fully mature figures.

Women's about 5' 5" to 5' 6" without shoes. Women's Petite under 5' 4" without shoes.

Sizes	18W/ US 16	20W/ US 18	22W/ US 20	24W/ US 22	26W/ US 24	28W/ US 26	30W/ US 28	32W / US 30	
Sizes – European	44	46	48	50	52	54	56	58	
Bust	40	42	44	46	48	50	52	54	in
Waist	33	35	37	39	41½	44	46½	49	in
Hip – 9 in below waist	42	44	46	48	50	52	54	56	in
Back waist length	17⅛	17¼	17⅜	17½	17⅝	17¾	17⅞	18	in
Petite – back waist length	16⅛	16¼	16⅜	16½	16⅝	16¾	16⅞	17	in

Unisex – For figures within Misses', Men's, Teen-Boys', Boys', and Girls' size ranges.

Sizes	XXS	XS	S	M	L	XL	XXL	
Chest/Bust	28-29	30-32	34-36	38-40	42-44	46-48	50-52	in
Hip	29-30	31-32½	35-37	39-41	43-45	47-49	51-53	in

Metric

Misses'/Miss Petite – For well-proportioned, developed figures.

Misses' about 165–168 cm without shoes. Miss Petite under 163 cm without shoes.

Sizes	4/ US 2	6/ US 4	8/ US 6	10/ US 8	12/ US 10	14/ US 12	16/ US 14	18/ US 16	20/ US 18	22/ US 20	24/ US 22	26/ US 24	
Sizes – European	30	32	34	36	38	40	42	44	46	48	50	52	
Bust	75	78	80	83	87	92	97	102	107	112	117	122	cm
Waist	56	58	61	64	67	71	76	81	87	94	99	106	cm
Hip – 23 cm below waist	80	83	85	88	92	97	102	107	112	117	122	127	cm
Back waist length	38.5	39.5	40	40.5	41.5	42	42.5	43	44	44	44.5	44.5	cm
Petite – back waist length	36	37	37.5	38	38.5	39.5	40	40.5	41.5	41.4	42	42	cm

Women's/Women's Petite – For the larger, more fully mature figures.

Women's about 165–168 cm without shoes. Women's Petite under 163 cm without shoes.

Sizes	18W/ US 16	20W/ US 18	22W/ US 20	24W/ US 22	26W/ US 24	28W/ US26	30W/ US 28	32W/ US 30	
Sizes – European	44	46	48	50	52	54	56	58	
Bust	102	107	112	117	122	127	132	137	cm
Waist	84	89	94	99	105	112	118	124	cm
Hip – 23 cm below waist	107	112	117	122	127	132	137	142	cm
Back waist length	43	44	44	44.5	45	45	45.5	46	cm
Petite – back waist length	40.5	41.5	41.5	42	42	42.5	42.5	43	cm

Unisex – For figures within Misses', Men's, Teen-Boys', Boys', and Girls' size ranges.

Sizes	XXS	XS	S	M	L	XL	XXL	
Bust	71-74	76-81	87-92	97-102	107-112	117-122	127-132	cm
Waist	74-76	79-83	89-94	99-104	109-114	119-124	130-135	cm

Reproduced with kind permission of Simplicity Patterns

Basic Techniques

HAND STITCHING

Today most hand stitching is used to mend, hem, apply badges, and prepare or finish off garments, unless you are using embroidery or cross stitch creatively. The basic stitches needed are therefore basting or gathering, tailor's tacks, slip stitch, back and running stitch, blanket stitch, and blind hem stitch.

RUNNING STITCH

The most common hand stitch, it is used to hold fabric layers together and has neat even stitches, approximately ⅛ in (3 mm) long with even gaps in between. Use all-purpose thread, approximately 16 in (40 cm) long. Secure the thread at one end with a knot or by taking 3–4 tiny stitches on the spot. Starting at the front of the work, pass the needle from front to back, then up to the front again in one pass. For speed, weave the needle in and out of the fabric 3–4 times in one go (diagram 1).

GATHERING STITCH

This is the same as the running stitch, but with slightly longer stitches, ¼–½ in (6–13 mm). It is used to pull up fabric into gathers or to attach a longer piece of fabric to a shorter piece. Use doubled thread for strength. Once stitched, pull up the thread to gather the fabric, adjust the folds and gathers evenly and then stitch 3–4 times on the spot to hold in place (diagram 2).

Diagram 1: Running stitch

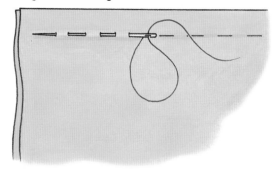

HELPFUL HINT:
When gathering long sections prevent the thread breaking or uneven gathering by separating the length into two or three sections and gather each separately.

Diagram 2: Gathering stitch

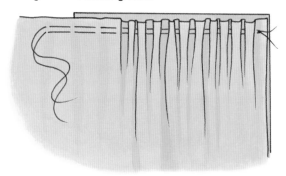

BASTING

Also known as tacking, basting is used to temporarily hold together two or more layers of fabric. There are two methods: pin basting (see threads and notions, page 37) and thread basting, which can be by machine or hand. Hand basting is the same process as the running stitch, using basting or all-purpose thread approximately 18 in (46 cm) long with knotted end and large ½ in (13 mm) stitches which will be removed later. (To remove, cut off the knot, then cut the thread at intervals and pull out. Remove before pressing.) To machine baste, set the sewing machine to the longest stitch length possible and stitch within the seam allowance.

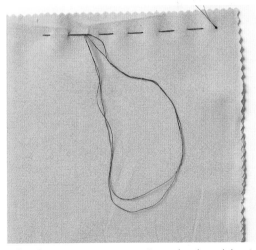

When basting, use a contrasting color thread that is easy to see and therefore to remove after stitching.

TAILOR'S TACKS

Traditionally used to mark placement points on fabric for pockets, zippers, darts, pleats, etc., they consist of 3–4 large, loopy hand stitches made through all layers, then carefully cut so that thread remains in each layer. To make a tailor's tack, use all-purpose thread, doubled.

- With tissue paper uppermost, take a stitch through the placement mark, through all layers, leaving a large loop of thread at the back and the thread tail at the front. Repeat three times. Cut off the thread, leaving the thread tail again.
- Unpin the tissue and snip through the loops on both sides, then carefully pull the fabric layers apart and snip the threads again so that the thread remains in both fabric layers.

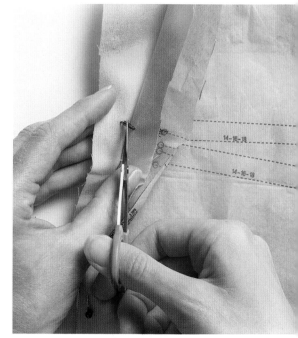

Snipping between the fabric layers

HELPFUL HINT:
Use a contrasting colored thread to denote different placement points, for example, blue for zipper placement, red for pleats.

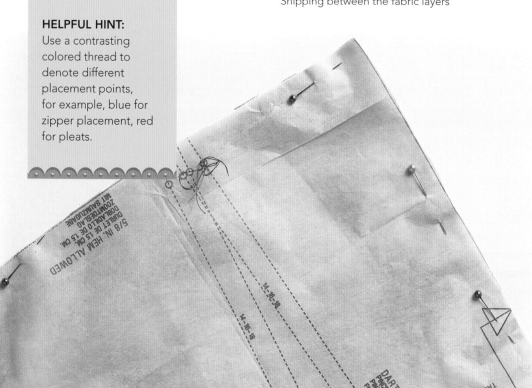

Completed tailor's tack

BACK STITCH

Similar to straight stitching by machine, back stitch by hand is the strongest of the hand seaming stitches as the stitches at the front of the work are close together and at the back they overlap slightly. As before, start with 3–4 stitches on the spot or a knot, then take a small backward stitch from front to back and up to front ⅛ in (3 mm) in front, all in one pass. For the next and subsequent stitches, stitch backward again, inserting the needle through to the back at the end of the first stitch, and up again ⅛ in (3 mm) in front (diagram 3).

Diagram 3: Back stitch

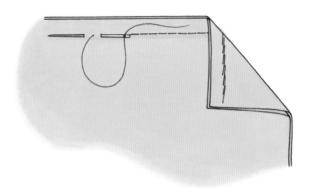

PRICK STITCH

Similar to back stitch, the stitches taken are tiny in order to be virtually invisible. Prick stitch is used on fabrics with a delicate texture or pile that might be spoiled with machine stitching. On the right side, the stitches are tiny and evenly spaced, while on the reverse they resemble back stitch. As with back stitch, secure the thread then take a backward stitch from front to back and up to front a very scant ¹⁄₁₆–⅛ in (2–3 mm) ahead. Go back to reverse just 2–3 fibers behind the first stitch and repeat (diagram 4).

Diagram 4: Prick stitch

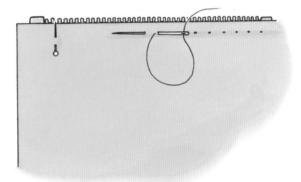

SLIP STITCH

Used to close gaps left to turn work to the right side or as a hemming technique, slip stitch is another stitch that should be virtually invisible. Use a thread to closely match the trim or fabric being stitched. Working from right to left, secure the thread then pull the needle through one folded edge, then a stitch of the same size through the other folded edge. Work along the gap, bringing the sides together (diagram 5). If hemming, take up just 1–2 fibers of the main fabric and a longer ¼ in (6 mm) stitch in the folded hem allowance.

Diagram 5: Slip stitch

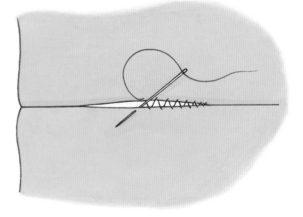

Whip stitch

WHIP STITCH

This is a strong overedge stitch, usually used to attach trims to soft furnishings or badges and motifs to garments. Use thread to match the trim or motif. Having secured the thread under the trim, bring the needle from the back of the main fabric through to the front of the trim, take over the trim edge and through to the main fabric, picking up 2–3 fibers only. Bring back through the trim, over the edge to the main fabric again.

OVERCAST STITCH

Similar to whip stitch, overcast stitch is used to finish raw edges. Bring the needle through from back to front of the fabric ⅛ in (3 mm) from the edge, then take over the edge to the back before coming through the fabric to the front again, a little to the left of the first stitch.

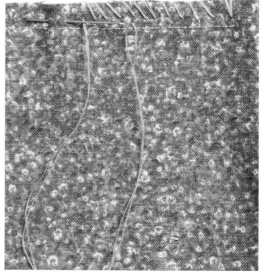

Overcast stitch

BLANKET STITCH

A decorative edge stitch used to finish the edges of blankets or throws on fabrics that do not fray, or to hold fabric edges together. On fabrics that fray, such as velvet, fold a double hem before blanket stitching over it. The stitch is often made using thicker thread or contrasting colored threads. Wool or fine ribbon can also be used. Having secured the thread at the back of the work, bring the needle through from back to front, ¼ in (6 mm) from the edge. With the needle only part way through, loop the thread round the needle before pulling it all the way through, pushing the loop to sit on the fabric edge. Again, take the needle from back through to front approximately ¼ in (6 mm) further along, loop the thread over the needle and pull through again. Continue along the edge. At corners, work three stitches into the same hole.

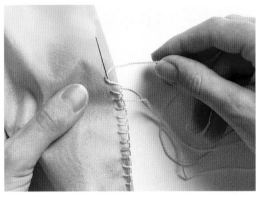

Blanket stitch

BLIND HEM STITCH

Hand-stitched blind hemming should be invisible from the right side of the fabric. It is made by taking small stitches in the main fabric and larger stitches in the hem allowance, which has been folded back so that no stitching shows from either side. In order to maintain a soft, rounded hem, avoid pressing the hem edge, just press the stitched area gently to embed the stitches.

- Fold the raw edge under at least ½ in (13 mm), then fold the hem allowance up and pin in position.
- Starting at one edge, secure the thread (color matched to fabric) in the hem allowance and then in the top of the hem allowance back on itself, in order to take a stitch approximately ¼ in (6 mm) from the fold.
- Next pick up one or two fibers from the main fabric before taking up a longer stitch in the folded hem allowance, approximately ⅜ in (1 cm) along the hem (diagram 6).

HELPFUL HINTS:
* For blanket stitch, draw a chalk stitching line ¼ in (6 mm) from the edge to keep the stitches even and neat.
* For blind hem stitch, to ensure absolutely no stitching is seen on the outside of the garment, fuse stay tape to the main fabric under the hem allowance and pick up fibers from the tape rather than the main fabric.

Diagram 6:
Blind hem stitch

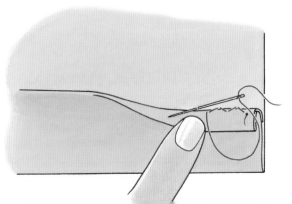

MACHINE STITCHING

There are a number of functional machine stitches used in dressmaking and soft furnishings, mostly based on a straight or zigzag stitch or a combination of both. These stitches are found on most sewing machines and are used for specific sewing techniques or finishes.

HELPFUL HINT:
To prevent threads tangling at the start of a seam, turn the fly wheel by hand until the needle comes back up with the bobbin thread looped with the top thread. Hold both thread tails behind the needle, start stitching about 1 in (2.5 cm) from the fabric edge, reverse to ⅝ in (1.5 cm) from the fabric edge then straight stitch again.

STRAIGHT STITCH

As the name suggests, this is a straight line of stitching, most commonly used to sew seams and join fabric layers together. An average stitch length for a medium-weight fabric is 2.5 mm (10 stitches per inch). Increase the stitch length when stitching on heavy or bulky fabrics and reduce it to sew finer fabrics. The amount of adjustment will depend on the thickness and number of layers so always test on a sample piece of fabric of the same weight, number of layers, and interfacing. If the seam starts to pucker, increase the stitch length slightly. If the fabric gathers easily and the stitches appear loose, reduce the stitch length slightly.

REVERSE STITCH

This is the same as straight stitch, but stitching backward. Usually achieved by holding down a button or lever on the sewing machine. It is used to fix stitching at the start and end of a seam. Zigzag stitch can also be stitched in reverse.

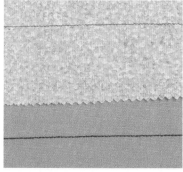

Examples of straight stitch

ZIGZAG STITCH

This stitch has both width and length directions, both of which can be altered to increase or decrease the stitch width or length. Width is altered to reduce stitch size from side to side. Length is altered to reduce the distance between the stitches. Zigzag stitch is used to stitch a flexible seam on stretch fabrics or finish raw edges. When finishing, stitch so the outer swing of the needle falls outside the raw edge.

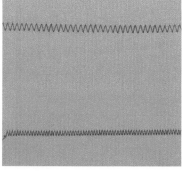

Zigzag stitch

VARIATIONS OF STRAIGHT STITCH

Machine basting – As with hand basting, this is used to hold fabric layers together temporarily. Stitches are removed once the seam is sewn. Use a contrasting color thread and do not fix stitch at the start or finish. Use the longest machine stitch length available and hold the fabric in front and behind the presser foot to prevent it gathering while being stitched. To remove basting, snip the basting stitches at intervals and then pull out the thread. Machine basting is useful when fitting skirts to waistbands, sleeves into armholes, collars onto neck edges, etc.

Gathering stitch – This is the same as machine basting but with a slightly shorter stitch. Guide the fabric loosely, allowing the fabric to gather as it is being stitched. Pull up the bobbin thread to gather further before tying the thread ends in a knot to secure.

Stay stitch – This is a row or line of stitching just inside the seam allowance – ½ in (13 mm) from the raw edge. Use a regular stitch length. Stay stitching is used to prevent bias-cut edges and curves, necklines, and shoulders from stretching too much while being handled.

HELPFUL HINT:
Stay stitch in the same direction as the fabric grain, which can be determined by "stroking the cat." Run a finger along the cut edge: as a cat's fur is smooth one way when stroked, so the fibers of the fabric will curl smoothly one way.

Diagram 1: Ease stitch

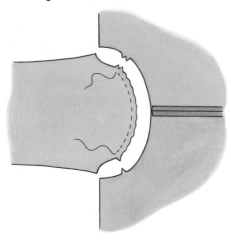

Diagram 1: Ease stitch

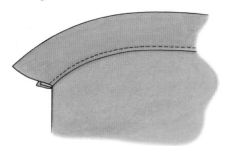

EASE STITCH

This is similar to a gathering stitch and stay stitch. Increase the stitch length to between ⅛–¼ in (3–5 mm), depending on the thickness of the fabric, and, if necessary, slightly loosen the needle tension so that the fabric gathers very, very slightly. Stitch within the seam allowance, close to the seam line. Ease stitch is used to fit slightly longer pieces of fabric to shorter lengths such as sleeves into sleeve heads without any gathers or folds appearing on the right side of the garment. Once stitched, match the notches and fit the eased section to the straight piece (diagram 1). If necessary, draw the bobbin thread of the ease stitching up slightly to improve the fit and distribute the fullness evenly. With the eased section uppermost, finish by machine stitching the pieces together.

Diagram 2: Under stitch

UNDER STITCH

A regular straight stitch, this is used on facings, etc., to prevent them rolling to the outside. Before under stitching, seam allowances should be graded and clipped (see paper patterns, page 47) and then pressed toward the facing. With the garment right side up and the facing held out, stitch through the facing and seam allowances, ⅛ in (3 mm) from the seam line. Fold the facing back inside and press with a press cloth (diagram 2).

HELPFUL HINT:
Use a stitching guide such as the edge of the fabric or the edge of the presser foot or mark a chalk line to ensure that the stitching remains an accurate distance from the edge.

TOP STITCH

This is quite simply stitching on top of the fabric to provide a decorative finish or as a functional aid to attach patch pockets, machine stitch hems, and keep facings and seam allowances flat. For straight rows, stitch with a slightly longer-than-usual stitch length (⅛–¼ in/3–5 mm), decreasing the length slightly when stitching around curves. If used for decorative purposes, use a contrasting colored thread.

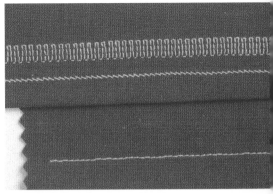

Top stitch

EDGE STITCH

Edge stitch is an extra row of stitching on the right side of the fabric, designed to be visible. It is similar to top stitch (see above) but is usually stitched much closer to the fold, seam, or finished edge (⅛ in/2–3 mm). It is usually stitched in matching thread. Edge stitching produces a crisp, neat edge and helps prevent facings and seam allowances from rolling out. Press the edges to be stitched. To keep the stitching accurate, use a zipper or clear plastic foot with the needle to the far right so that the foot holds the fabric.

If you are a beginner or unsure of your stitching accuracy, leave it out.

Edge stitch

STITCH IN THE DITCH

This is the term used to describe a line of straight stitching sewn within the seam in order to hold facings, casings, seam allowances, and bindings in place on the reverse. With facings or bindings in place, work from the right side. Spread the seam open by holding either side of the presser foot and then stitching in the ditch created, catching the facing or binding in place on the reverse. The fabric will roll back slightly over the ditch and hide the stitches (diagram 3).

Diagram 3: Stitch in the ditch

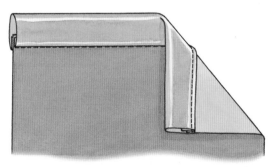

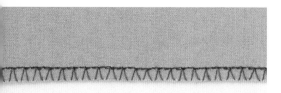

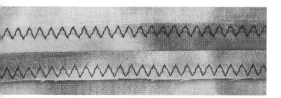

Overcast edge

Three-step zigzag stitch

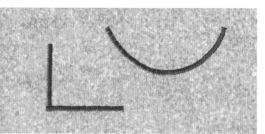

Stretch stitch

Satin stitch

VARIATIONS OF ZIGZAG STITCH

Overcast – Using the zigzag stitch option, overcast stitch is used to finish raw edges of fabric. Stitch with the fabric edge placed so the right swing of the needle falls off the fabric. For heavier fabrics, increase the stitch length and width and for lightweight fabrics, decrease the stitch width. If fabrics fray easily, overcast the fabric edges before stitching the seams.

Three-step zigzag stitch – Also known as tricot stitch, this is another zigzag stitch used to finish edges. The zigzags are made in three stitches, hence the name. It provides a flatter finish than regular zigzag stitch. Stitch close to the raw edge of the trimmed seam (not overlapping).

Stretch stitch – Used to stitch stretchy fabrics, this is a flexible stitch that is worked with two stitches forward and one back so that each stretch stitch is stitched three times. This creates a flexible seam that will stretch with the fabric. Many modern sewing machines have a choice of stretch stitches. Adjust the stitch length and width to suit the fabric (longer for heavy fabrics, smaller for lightweight fabrics).

Satin stitch – Used to cover raw edges and to attach appliqué, this is a very close zigzag stitch. Many modern machines have it as a utility stitch, but if not, set the machine for zigzag stitch and the stitch length to a minimum of 0.45. Reduce the stitch width to suit the fabric – narrow for smaller stitches and lightweight work and wider for heavier fabric or appliqué.

HELPFUL HINT:
Many of the zigzag-based stitches are difficult to unpick and can leave holes, so always test different stitches on a sample of the same fabric with the same number of layers and interfacings.

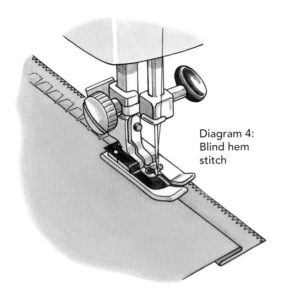

Diagram 4:
Blind hem
stitch

BLIND HEM STITCH

This is a very neat hemming stitch which produces a softly rounded hem finish. When stitched by machine, a small ladder-like stitch is visible on the right side of the fabric. To minimize this, use matching thread. The stitch is formed by catching just a tiny amount in the garment and two or three stitches in the hem allowance. Finish the raw edge before turning the hem allowance to the wrong side. Attach a blind hem foot, which has a metal guide and a shorter right toe, and place the fabric under the foot with the fold against the fabric guide. Ensure the needle just pierces the folded fabric close to the fold by adjusting the stitch width (diagram 4).

SHELL TUCK STITCH

Another hemming stitch, this is mainly used on bias-cut fabrics, knits, or soft, woven fabrics. Similar to blind hem stitch, it combines two or three straight stitches with a zigzag stitch. Sew along the fold so the needle on the right swing is clear of the fold to form the tucks.

HEIRLOOM STITCHING

This term encompasses many decorative stitches that are traditionally associated with heirloom projects such as christening gowns or table linen. Special needles are often used to help with the stitch effect, such as double or wing needles. Wing needles have a wider eye and are designed to leave holes as they stitch.

Shell tuck stitch

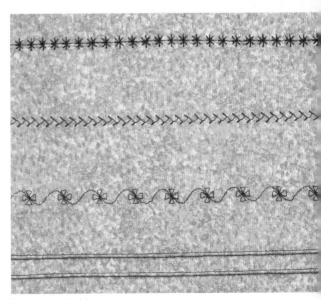

Heirloom stitching

CORNERS AND CURVES

Sooner or later you will come across projects that mean you have to sew curves or corners. There are some easy steps to take to handle them most effectively in order to produce a perfectly stitched, neat finish.

CORNERS

Seams at corners often take extra pressure and need to be strengthened. Unless handled properly, it can be difficult to achieve a neat, crisp corner because of bulky fabrics.

Fabric corners

Strengthening

Stitch with a regular stitch length to within 1 in (2.5 cm) of the corner, then reduce the stitch by 1/32 in (0.5–1 mm), depending on the fabric thickness, and stitch to the corner. Stop with the needle down, raise the presser foot, pivot the work slightly and then take 1–2 stitches diagonally across the corner. Raise the presser foot to pivot the work again, ready for the next seam. Stitch for 1 in (2.5 cm) before increasing the stitch length to a regular length again. Repeat for each corner (diagram 1).

Reducing bulk

Trim the seam allowance diagonally across the corner. If the fabric frays easily, dab on some fabric glue or fray check and allow to dry before turning the corner out. For very sharp corners, cut the corner off diagonally and then cut wedges at the start of either seam to grade the bulk at the corner when turned through (diagram 2).

Diagram 1: Strengthening

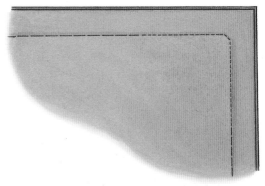

Diagram 2: Reducing bulk

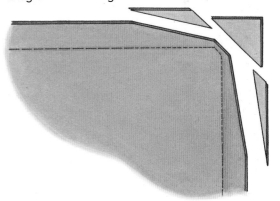

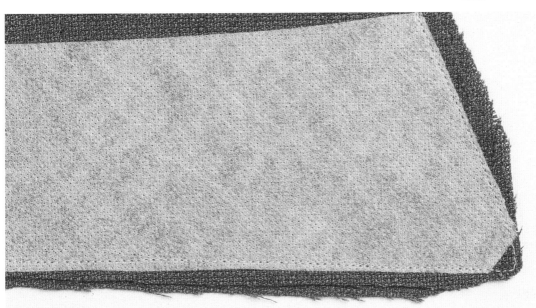

Reducing bulk

Mitered corner

Mitering

This is used to provide a neat, angled corner for patch pockets, hem edges, borders, and trims. Mitering corners also reduces bulk by cutting away some of the excess fabric. For a crisp mitered corner, follow these instructions:

- On either side of the corner, fold the seam allowances of both edges to the wrong side and press.
- Unfold and then refold the corner diagonally where the two creases cross, again to the wrong side. Press to make a crease (diagram 3).
- Unfold and then refold the fabric diagonally to bring the side edges together. Stitch across the diagonal. Trim the fabric close to the stitching and press the seam open.
- Turn the corner to the right side, using a point turner to push the corner out from the inside.

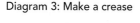

Diagram 3: Make a crease

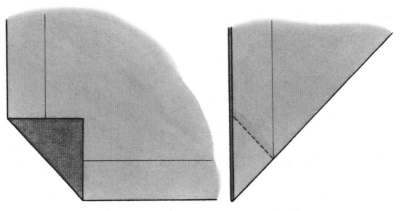

CURVES

Fabric cut on the curve will have at least part of the edge cut on the grain, which means the fabric will be more stretchy. To prevent unwanted stretch at shoulders, neck edges, or armholes, stay stitch (see machine stitching, page 65) or add bias tape, a fusible curved tape that is fused within the seam allowance to prevent stretch.

To ensure curved areas lie flat when turned through to the right side, seam allowances need to be clipped or notched so they can overlap or spread. Outer (convex) curves are notched by taking small wedge shapes from the seam allowance at regular intervals, while inner curves only need small clips cut into the seam allowance (diagram 4).

Diagram 4: Clip inner curve

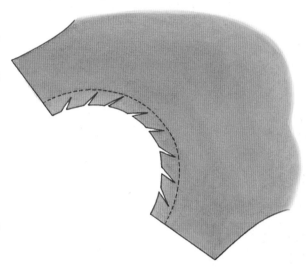

Notched outer curve

SEAMS

There are various seams that can be used to sew fabric layers together. Which to use depends on the fabric type and weight and the purpose of the seam.

GENERAL SEWING TIPS

Whatever seam technique used, there are a few steps to take to ensure perfect seaming every time:

- Before working on a project, try out the stitch technique on a fabric sample with the same number of layers and interfacings.
- Stitch all seams in the same direction, i.e., from top to bottom to prevent the fabric pulling and twisting in opposite directions.
- Once stitched, press the seams from both wrong and right side to embed the stitches. Always press before enclosing or crossing the seam with another row of stitching.

- Take care to maintain an even seam allowance (normally ⅝ in [1.5 cm] on garments and ¼ in [6 mm] on crafts). Seam allowances are provided to allow for adjustments and to prevent seams ripping apart during wear. Use the stitching guidelines on the throat plate (diagram 1). Most are marked in ⅛-in (3-mm) increments. Alternatively, use the edge of the presser foot or use masking tape to mark your own guide. On close-fitting garments or patchwork projects, mark the stitching line with a chalk pencil to ensure total accuracy.

Diagram 1: Throat plate

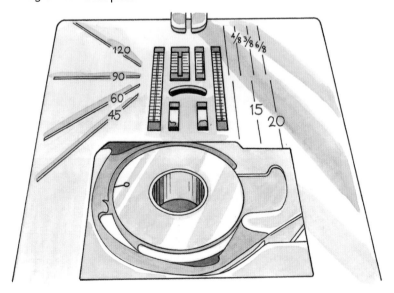

HELPFUL HINT:
Avoid threads tangling at the start of a seam by holding both the bobbin and top thread tails behind the needle. Start approximately 1 in (2.5 cm) from the top of the fabric, stitch forward ½ in (13 mm) and then reverse to within ⅝ in (1.5 cm) of the top of the fabric before continuing forward again.

PLAIN SEAM

This is the most commonly used seam for woven fabrics, stitched with a straight stitch, usually ⅝ in (1.5 cm) from the raw edges. The stitch length depends on the fabric thickness and number of layers being seamed together. For lightweight fabrics use between 2–2.5 mm (10–12 spi), for medium-weight fabric 2.5–3 mm (8–10 spi), and for heavyweight fabrics between 3–4.5 mm (6–8 spi).

Plain seam

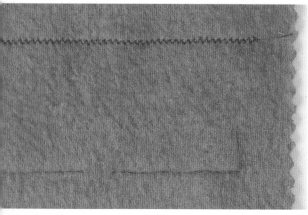

Stretch fabric with zigzag stitching and broken straight stitching

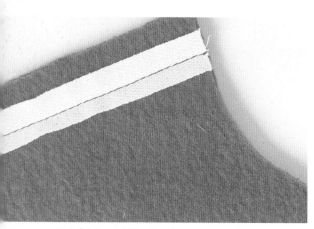

Knit fabric stabilized with stay tape

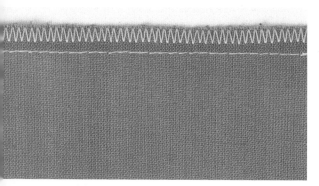

Double stitched seam

KNIT SEAMS

Fabrics that stretch and need to remain flexible need seams that stretch also and thus should be stitched with a zigzag stitch of some sort. Use a regular zigzag stitch, three-step zigzag, or a stretch stitch. All can have the length and width altered to make the stitching wider and further apart. For lightweight fabrics choose a smaller length and width, and for heavier fabrics, a wider stitch length and width.

On some areas of knit fabrics – such as necklines and shoulders – it is necessary to prevent unwanted stretch. Stitch these areas with a straight stitch. For very stretchy fabrics, add stay tape in the seam allowance (see Interfacings and stabilizers, page 39), which gives the fabric more stability, then stitch the seam with a straight stitch.

DOUBLE STITCHED SEAM

This is used to strengthen the seam in stretch fabrics or to stitch and finish laces and sheer fabrics. In stretch fabrics, the extra row of stitching prevents the fabric curling. Stitch the first row along the seam line, using a straight stitch. Stitch the second row a scant ⅛ in (3 mm) away, stitching in the same direction, using either a straight or small zigzag stitch. Trim close to the outer stitching.

BIAS SEAMS

Again, bias-cut fabric has more stretch and thus has to be treated with care. To avoid rippling seams or unwanted stretch, stitch slowly, holding the fabric in front and behind the presser foot, slightly stretching it as you sew. Once carefully pressed, the stitching relaxes into a smooth seam. Heavier-weight fabrics also need stabilizing to prevent them drooping and sagging. To do this, add stay tape to the seam allowance.

FRENCH SEAM

Ideal for sheers, lightweight fabrics, blinds, and
unlined curtains where the reverse is visible. French
seams are created with two rows of straight
stitching, first with the fabric wrong sides together,
then with the fabric refolded right sides together.
Stitch the first seam ⅜ in (1 cm) from the raw edges,
trim to a scant ⅛ in (3 mm), and press. Turn the fabric
so the right sides are together and the seam is on
the fold, then stitch again in the same direction, ¼ in
(6 mm) from the edge (diagram 2).

French seam

Diagram 2: Stitch again in the same direction

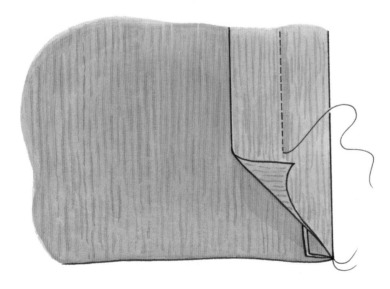

Lapped seam

LAPPED SEAM

This is perfect for fabrics that don't fray, such as faux suedes, leathers, and fleece. The fabric is overlapped rather than sewn with right sides together. Again two rows of straight stitching are used. On the fabric that will overlap, mark the stitching line with chalk (see diagram 3), then trim the seam allowance away to within ⅟₁₆–⅛ in (2–3 mm) of this marked line. Place the cut edge over the other fabric piece, so that the marked stitching line just overlaps the stitching line of the under piece (note both pieces are right sides up). Stitch the first row along the marked stitching line. Stitch again, in the same direction, ¼–½ in (6–13 mm) from the first row, catching the seam allowance of the under piece in the stitching (diagram 3).

Diagram 3: Catch the seam allowance of the under piece

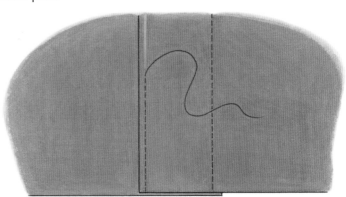

HELPFUL HINT:
Lap vertical seams away from the center and horizontal seams down. Avoid using pins on fabrics that mark – use double-sided basting tape instead.

WELT AND DOUBLE WELT SEAMS

Similar to lapped seams, welt seams are particularly suitable for heavyweight fabrics. Again the seam is formed with two rows of straight stitching. The first is a regular seam with right sides together, the second is to catch the seam allowance. Having stitched the seam, grade the seam allowances, which reduces bulk, by trimming the under seam allowance to ¼ in (6 mm). Then, working from the right side, sew again ¼–½ in (6–13 mm) from the seam, catching the untrimmed seam allowance in the stitching. This will encase the trimmed seam allowance at the same time (diagram 4). A double welt seam has another row of stitching close to the seam line.

Welt seam

Diagram 4: Encase the trimmed seam allowance

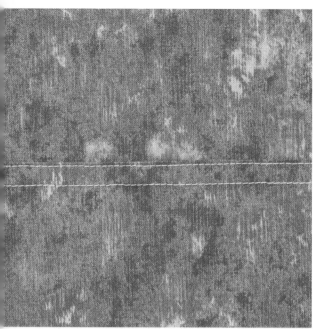

Flat fell seam

FLAT FELL SEAM

Used on sportswear and simple reversible garments, this seam technique sews and finishes the seam allowances, with the seam allowances on the right side of the fabric. As with French seams, stitch a regular seam with the wrong sides together then press the seam allowances together to one side. Trim the under seam allowance to ⅛ in (3 mm). Tuck under the raw edge of the upper seam allowance and press in place (if preferred, baste in place), then stitch close to the fold from the right side.

Diagram 5: Sew and finish seam allowances

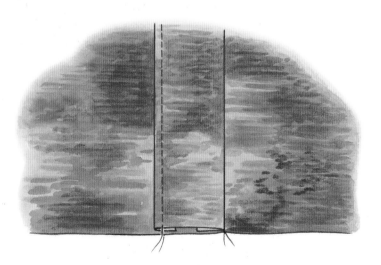

SEAM FINISHES

Unless seams are encased, they need to be finished to prevent the fabric fraying during wear and to reduce bulk in the seam area. As with seaming, there are different methods to finish seams, depending on the type of fabric being stitched.

REDUCING BULK

Although they do not need finishing, seam allowances that are encased may need to be reduced in order to reduce the bulk within the seam area. This can be done by clipping and notching (see paper patterns, page 47), trimming, and grading. Grading is simply cutting the two seam allowances to a different width which cuts down the bulk of the fabric and prevents unsightly ridges showing through on the right side. Trim the seam allowance closest to the main fabric to ¼ in (6 mm) and the under seam allowance to ⅛ in (3 mm) (diagram 1).

Diagram 1: Grading

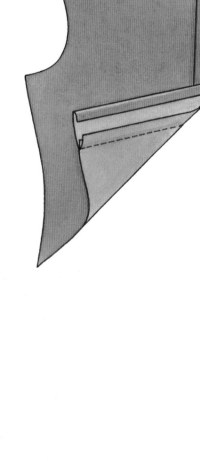

PINKED EDGES

The quickest way to finish cottons and other lightweight fabrics is to cut the edges with pinking shears to within ¼ in (6 mm) of the seam. Press before and after cutting.

CLEAN FINISHING

Press open the seam allowance then turn under the raw edges by ⅛ in (3 mm) and stitch in place with a straight stitch. This is suitable for light- to medium-weight fabrics.

Pinked seam edge

OVERCAST OR ZIGZAG SEAM FINISH

This method involves using a zigzag stitch on woven fabric so the right swing of the stitch is just off the fabric edge. On knit fabrics, keep all the stitches on the seam allowance, then trim the seam allowance close to the stitching. Lightweight fabrics can have both seam allowances finished together as one. On heavier-weight fabrics, press the seam allowances open and finish separately.

BOUND SEAMS

These are often used in tailored garments, particularly if the inside might be visible. Seam allowances are bound with bias binding tape or special tricot seam binding tape that folds in two, encasing the raw edges. Use a straight stitch on woven fabrics and a zigzag stitch on knit fabrics. Stitch through the tape and seam allowance, catching both the top and underside of the tape at the same time.

TOP STITCHED SEAM

This is a seam finish that can be functional or decorative. It helps make the seam more durable as well as provides a crisp edge. For a decorative finish, use contrasting threads and any decorative stitch. For simple top stitching, use matching thread and a straight stitch. If sewing lightweight fabrics, press the finished seam allowances together to one side, then, working from the right side, top stitch ¼ in (6 mm) from the edge, catching the seam allowance in the stitching. For heavier-weight fabrics, press the seam allowances open and top stitch from the right side down both sides of the seam.

Seams bound with bias binding tape and tricot seam binding tape

Top stitched seam and double top stitched seam

Style Techniques

HEMMING

There are a number of different ways to hem and different styles of hem. The main hemming techniques used in dressmaking are covered here.

GENERAL TIPS

1. Let a garment or curtains hang for 24 hours before hemming to allow the fabric to settle and drop. This is particularly important for garments cut on the bias or knit and loosely woven fabrics.

2. Apart from finishing off a garment or curtain, hems can help the drape by adding weight. Hem depths vary depending on the garment. As a guide, for straight dresses, skirts, and coats, allow 2–3 in (5–7.5 cm). For trousers and flared and A-line hems, allow 1¼–2 in (3–5 cm). Hems on curtains depend on fabric thickness and length of curtain and range from 2–6 in (5–15 cm).

3. Measure for length from the floor to desired length. Wear appropriate shoes to ensure the back and front are even.

4. To mark the hemline, place pins horizontally or mark with chalk.

5. Turn the hem allowance to the wrong side along the marked hem edge and pin at right angles close to the fold. Trim the hem allowance (see average hem depths above) (diagram 1). Working from the wrong side, turn the hem allowance up at the marked hemline, matching side seams. Insert pins at right angles close to the folded edge. If it is uneven, trim the hem allowance to the depth required.

Diagram 1: Trim the hem allowance

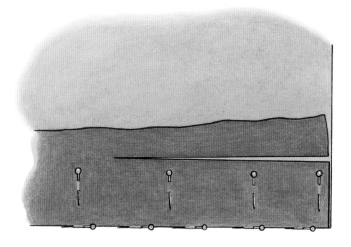

Easing in fullness on curved hem

6. Always try garments on again when the hem is pinned in place before stitching, again wearing the appropriate shoes.

7. Garments which are A-line or have a curved hem will have extra fullness that needs to be eased in to prevent ridges and folds at the hem. Ease stitch ¼ in (6 mm) from the raw hem edge and then gently pull up the bobbin thread to very slightly gather the excess. Spread it evenly and pin in place.

8. Choose a hem finish that is appropriate for the project – i.e., fluted lettuce hems on knit or very lightweight transparent fabrics, bound hems on tailored suits, jackets, and coats, blind hems on medium-weight fabrics, and rolled hems on lightweight fabrics.

9. Having determined the correct hem allowance, finish the raw edge on fabrics that ravel (fabrics that don't fray such as knits and fleece don't need finishing). On lightweight cottons, pink the edge with pinking sheers. On other fabrics, overcast or zigzag stitch or serge the edge. Turn up and finish by the preferred method (see following pages).

HEM FINISHES

Double hemming

Fold the hem allowance up, folding it again so the raw edge meets the first fold (diagram 2). Either top stitch or blind hem in place depending on the fabric weight and garment style. As the raw edge is encased, it is not necessary to finish it.

Diagram 2: Fold hem allowance up

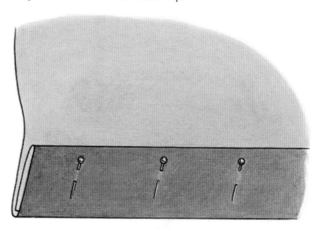

Top stitched hem

As with other top stitching, the stitches show on the right side. Suitable for lightweight fabrics and casual clothes, this is a quick hemming finish. Make a double hem as above (stretch knit fabrics and fleece can be folded once), then, working from the right side, stitch close to the inner fold. On heavier-weight fabrics, fold up the hem allowance then tuck the raw edge under ⅜ in (1 cm), rather than make a double hem. Again top stitch close to the inner fold, working from the right side. Raw edges do not need finishing as they are enclosed within the stitching. To simulate a cover stitch hem (serger technique), stitch two parallel rows in the same direction or stitch with a widely spaced twin needle.

Top stitched hems – twin and narrow stitching

Rolled hem

Ideal for lightweight and sheer fabrics, the hem allowance is minimal and thus doesn't look unsightly from the right side. If possible use a rolled hem presser foot through which the fabric is fed and rolled as it is stitched. If not, mark the hem length plus a hem allowance of just ⅛ in (3 mm). Fold up the hem and very lightly press. Stitch as close to the fold as possible, then trim away any excess hem allowance. Fold the hem again along the stitching, rolling the stitches just inside the hem and stitch again close to the inner fold.

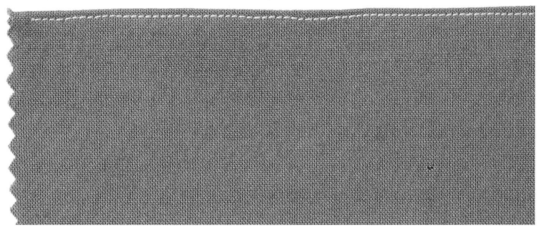

Rolled hem

Lettuce hemming

Similar to rolled hems, lettuce or fluted hems look pretty on lightweight stretch fabrics. Prepare the hem allowance as for rolled hems, then using a small, close zigzag stitch, with the right swing of needle falling off the fabric, pull the fabric taut in front and behind the machine to stretch it as you sew. Alternatively use a serger with a slightly tightened needle tension, again stretching the fabric as you sew.

Lettuce hemming

Blind hemming

Virtually invisible, blind hems are ideal for medium- and heavyweight fabrics, smart separates, and suits. A machine stitched blind hem will leave a tiny ladder-like row of stitches on the right side. Use a thread to match the fabric to reduce visibility. Prepare the hem allowance as above, then fold the hem allowance to the wrong side before folding it back on itself so that ¼ in (6 mm) of the finished hem edge is to the right of the fold. Use a blind hem foot, with the metal guard on the foot running alongside the fold. The blind hem stitch is a straight stitch (in the hem allowance) with a single left swing into the garment every few stitches (diagram 3). Once finished, fold the hem back out and press the stitching – do not press the hem edge as blind hems should have a rounded finish.

Blind hemming on a sewing machine

Diagram 3: Blind hem stitch

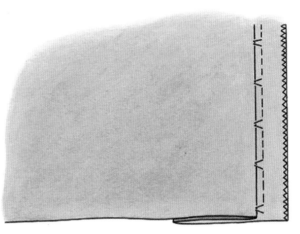

Taped hems

These provide a neat finish on garments where the hem might be seen, such as jackets and coats, or to extend the length of a garment. Use bias binding, ribbon, or lace edging. To determine the amount of tape needed, measure the circumference of the garment and add 5 in (13 cm) for curves, corners, and overlapping ends. Machine stitch the binding to the right side of the hem allowance ¼ in (6 mm) from the edge. Fold up the hem at the hemline and then hand stitch the tape in place with blind hem stitch (see hand stitching, page 63).

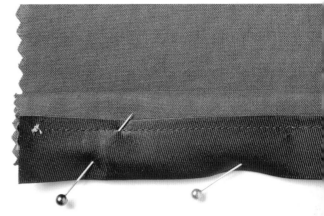

Taped hem

Leather or suede hems

To avoid stitching leather and suede, use fusible hemming web. Reduce the hem allowance to a maximum of ⅝ in (1.5 cm) by trimming off the excess. Turn up the hem on the hemline and place the webbing between the fabric layers. Using a press cloth, press with a medium-hot dry iron. On heavyweight leathers, simply cut the hem at the hemline and leave unfinished.

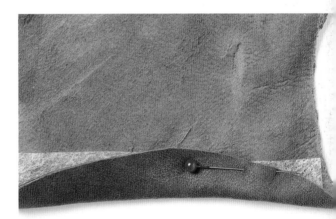

Leather hem with webbing

Tailored hems

Tailored hems require a crisp finish, achieved by adding a strip of interfacing within the hem allowance. If sewing medium- or heavyweight fabrics, the drape and hang is helped with the addition of dress weights. These metal disks or lengths of chain are added to the hem allowance at the sides and front edges prior to final hemming.

Linings

Usually stitched with a top stitched double hem, lining hems should finish above the main garment or curtain hemline, ideally so the lining finishes at the top of the hem allowance on the main fabric.

Tailored hem with interfacing and dress weights

FACINGS AND BANDS

Facings and bands are used to neaten and finish garments at the neck, armhole, and front and back openings. Usually cut from the same fabric as the garment, they are interfaced for added stability and then stitched, right sides together, to the garment edge before being turned to the inside.

Some jacket and coat designs have self-faced front openings, where the facing is cut as one with the jacket front and then folded back on itself to form the facing.

HANDLING TIPS

- Neck facings are generally curved, so they are cut across the grain and thus are prone to stretching. To prevent unwanted stretch, stay stitch the neck edge of the garment and the facing, stitching a normal stitch length just inside the seam allowance – ½ in (13 mm) from the raw edge (diagram 1).

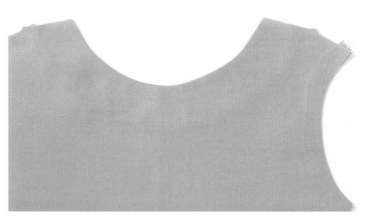

Garment front with facings at neck and armhole

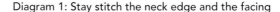

Diagram 1: Stay stitch the neck edge and the facing

HELPFUL HINT:
When working with bulky, thick fabrics, cut facings from a lighter-weight lining or cotton to reduce bulk at the neck, armhole, or front.

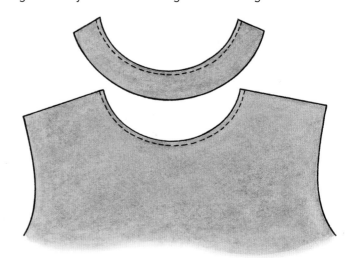

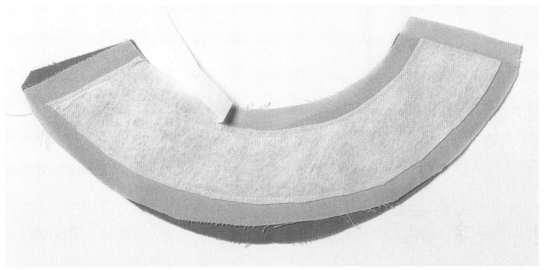

Sew-in interfacing trimmed after sewing

- Facings are interfaced over the whole piece whereas bands are interfaced along half the width. Trim fusible interfacing so that it fits just inside the seam line. After stitching the sew-in interfacing in place, trim close to the stitching to eliminate bulk from the seams.
- Bands are generally straight strips of fabric, cut along the straight of grain and folded in half lengthwise. Only half of the strip needs interfacing. As with facings, cut the fusible interfacing to sit just inside the seam line and butting against the fold line. Band width is a personal choice and depends on the garment style – kimonos, dressing gowns, and coats suit a wider band, 4–6 in (10–15 cm) folded to 2–3 in (5–8 cm), whereas jackets suit narrow bands of 1–2 in (2.5–5 cm), folded to ¼–1 in (6–25 mm).
- Finish the outer edge of the facing or band prior to sewing to the garment by turning the raw edge under and top stitching in place. Alternatively, use overcast stitch or serge the edge. Fabrics that don't ravel, such as fleece and stretch knits, do not need finishing.

- After stitching the facing or bands to the garment, right sides together, grade the seam allowances, trimming the garment edge to ¼ in (6 mm) and the facing to ⅛ in (3 mm). Clip and notch the curved areas, which will help the facing or band lay flat when turned through (diagram 2). Press with the seam allowance pressed toward the facing.
- To help prevent the facing from rolling out, under stitch the seam allowances to the facing

Diagram 2: Clip and notch curved areas

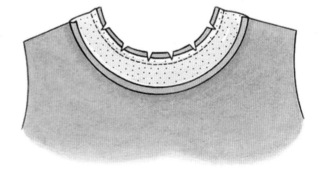

only by opening out the facing and stitching close to edge, catching the seam allowances in the stitching (see machine stitching, page 66). Turn the facing to the inside, rolling between thumb and fingers so the seam line falls just inside the edge. Press.

- To hem a band, stitch right sides together to the garment, fold the band in half lengthwise, again right sides together, and stitch across the ends from the fold to the raw edges (diagram 3). Trim the seam allowance and turn through. At the hem edge, stitch across the end the same depth as the hem allowance on the garment.

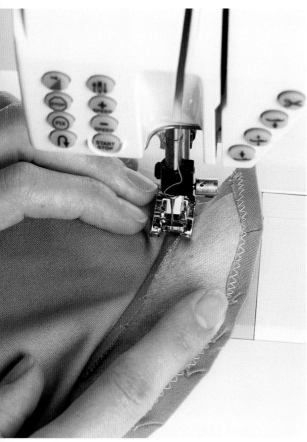

Understitching the seam allowances

Diagram 3: Hem a band

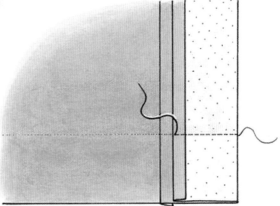

DARTS

Darts help mold fabric to fit at the bust, waist, and shoulders. They transform a flat piece of fabric into a figure-fitting garment.

A dart is usually wide at one end and tapered at the other (hence the name). When folded to the wrong side, it reduces the amount of fabric. Double-ended darts are used at the waistline to shape the waist and are tapered to a point at either end, with the widest section in the middle. Generally stitched in a straight line from point to widest part, darts are also occasionally stitched with a curved line for a closer fit.

Transfer any dart placement lines from the pattern to the wrong side of the fabric using chalk, pencil, or tailor's tacks. If you are creating your own pattern, add darts for shaping at the bust and waist.

Fabric piece with darts marked

BUST DARTS

Start just below the armhole at the side seam, tapering to a point 1 in (2.5 cm) from the fullest part of the bust. The top line of the dart is straight and the lower line angled up to complete the shaping. The dart size at the widest part is the difference between the bust at the fullest point and the chest measurement (taken under the arms, just above the bust). For very full busts, a further dart from the waist to the mid-bust point can also be added (diagram 1).

WAIST DARTS

These are placed midway between the center of the waist and the side seam, tapering to a point just above the hip (diagram 2). The amount of fabric to be folded into a dart at the widest point should not be more than 2½ in (6.5 cm), folding to 1¼ in (3 cm). To determine the dart size, divide the difference between the hip and the waist measurements by the number of darts being used (usually two at the front and two at the back). If the difference is 10 in (25 cm), the amount to be folded out will be 2½ in (6.5 cm) per dart.

Diagram 1: Darts for full busts

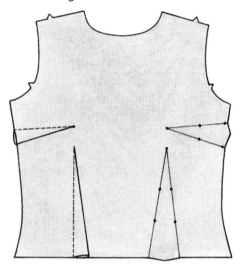

Diagram 2: Waist darts

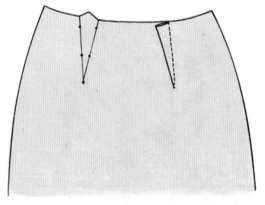

HELPFUL HINT:
Use a chalk pencil to draw the stitching line from the widest part to the point.

Stitching darts

1. Fold the fabric right sides together at the dart placement, matching the widest dart positions and tapering the fold to nothing at the point. Pin in place.

2. Stitch from the point on the fold toward the wide end of the dart. Secure the ends of the stitching with a lock or fix stitch or leave the thread tails and tie a knot at the end. Do not backstitch as this may cause a ridge in the fabric. Press the stitching and then press the dart fold toward the center if a vertical dart, and down toward the waist if a horizontal dart.

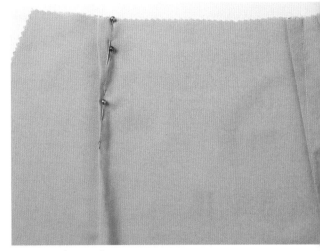

Pinning a dart in place

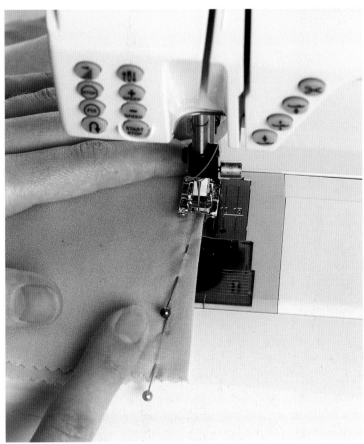

Stitching from the point on the fold

Diagram 3: Press dart seams open

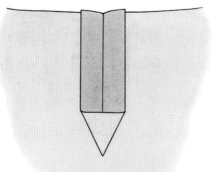

Diagram 4:
Clip into fold

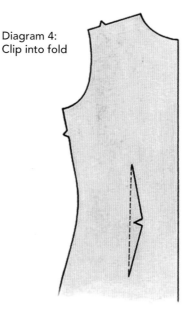

3. On heavyweight and thick fabrics such as fleece, cut the dart open along the fold, cutting as close to the point as possible. Press the dart seams open (diagram 3).

4. Fold the dart in the usual way and then machine stitch, starting at the center, working toward the point at one end. Start at the center again, overlapping a few stitches, then stitch to the other end. Again fix stitch or tie the ends rather than reverse stitch. Press to embed the stitches and then press the fold toward the center.

POCKETS

There are three styles of pocket that can be added quite simply – patch pockets, inseam pockets, and hip line (jean style). If using commercial paper patterns, pockets are included in the pattern pieces and instructions.

PATCH POCKETS

Formed from fashion fabric, these can be square, rectangular, or have shaped ends. They are stitched on top of the garment. The easiest method is to self-line the pockets. Determine the pocket size and then cut the pocket shape double the length plus seam allowances of ⅝ in (1.5 cm) all round.

Fold the pocket in half, so the fold is at the top of the pocket, with the fabric right sides together. Stitch the sides and bottom, leaving a turning gap in the center of the bottom edge (diagram 1). Trim the seam allowances, cutting the corners at angles and turn through. Slip stitch the opening and then press. If desired, top stitch ¼–½ in (6–13 mm) from the top edge. Attach to the garment by edge stitching along the sides and bottom.

Diagram 1: Stitch sides and bottom

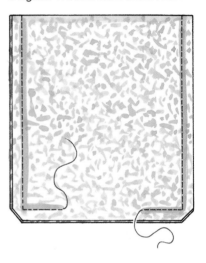

HELPFUL HINT:
Reinforce the top side edges by stitching in a small triangle as shown here.

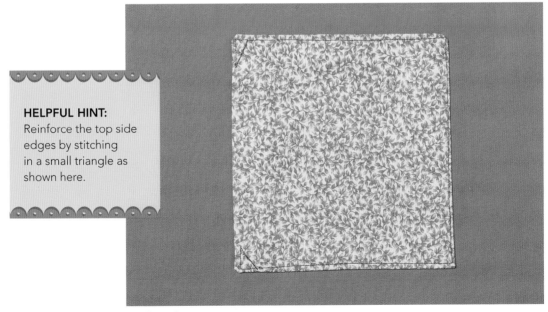

Patch pocket

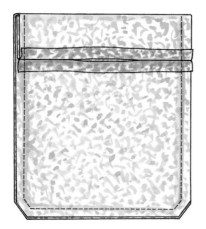

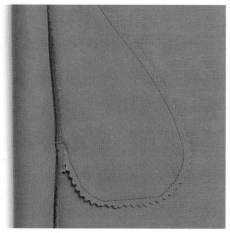

Inseam pocket

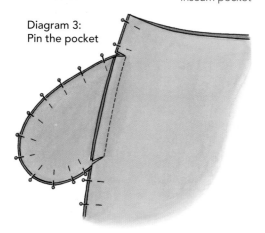

Diagram 3:
Pin the pocket

Lined patch pockets

If working with thick or bulky fabrics, it may be preferable to line the pockets with lining fabric. Cut the pocket to size plus seam allowances of ⅝ in (1.5 cm) at the sides and bottom and 1½ in (3 cm) on the top edge in both the main and lining fabrics. Mark the fold line 1½ in (3 cm) from the top. Pin the lining to the main fabric, right sides together, along the top edge and stitch, taking a ¼ in (6 mm) seam allowance and leaving a turning gap in the center.

At the marked fold line, fold the pocket top toward the lining by 1 in (2.5 cm), pin and stitch the sides and bottom. Then trim the seam allowances and clip the corners at an angle before turning through the opening in the top (diagram 2). Slip stitch the opening and press. If desired, top stitch the pocket opening before positioning on the garment and edge stitching the sides and bottom.

INSEAM POCKETS

Generally found in the side seams of trousers, skirts, and casual jackets, these pockets are attached to the front and back garment sections at the side edges and then the pocket bag is stitched at the same time as the side seam. They can be made from fashion fabric or lining, depending on the fabric weight.

The pocket shape is similar to a gloved hand, with a straight edge to attach to garment side approximately 3 in (8 cm) below the waist. With the right sides together, pin the straight edge of the pocket to the side seam and then machine stitch, taking the usual ⅝ in (1.5 cm) seam allowance. Finish and press the seam allowance toward the pocket. Repeat with the other pocket section and trouser or skirt back.

With right sides together, pin the front to the back, with the pocket extending beyond the seam, pinning around the pocket bag and down the side (diagram 3). Machine stitch, pivoting at the top and bottom of the pocket. Clip the seam allowance top and bottom of the pocket before pressing the pocket toward the front of the garment.

HIP LINE POCKETS

Also known as side slant pockets, these are shaped front pockets often found on jean-style trousers and skirts. They have two pocket parts, the facing and pocket back. The pocket facing can be cut from lining if the main fabric is thick or bulky.

Having cut the pocket sections, reinforce the opening edge of the pocket facing by stay stitching or adding stay tape or interfacing. Then with right sides together, stitch the facing to the garment front (diagram 4). Grade and clip the seam allowance. As extra reinforcement, press, then stitch the clipped seam allowance toward the pocket facing and under stitch (see machine stitching, page 66). Turn the facing to the inside along the seam line and press. If desired, top or edge stitch close to the fold.

Again with right sides together, machine stitch the pocket facing to the pocket back around the outer edge (diagram 5). Finish the raw edges with zigzag stitch. Then pin and stitch the garment side seam, catching the straight edge of the pocket bag side in the seam. The top of the pocket bag will then be caught in the waistband seaming.

Hip line pocket

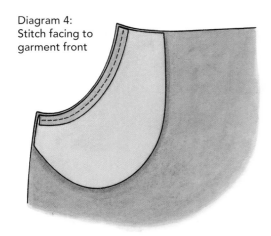

Diagram 4:
Stitch facing to
garment front

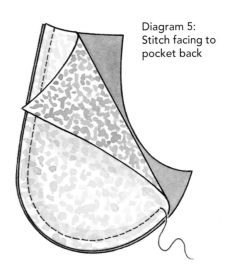

Diagram 5:
Stitch facing to
pocket back

WAISTBANDS

Waistbands add a reinforced, stable section of fabric from which trousers or skirts hang and finish off the top of the garment.

Waistbands can have front, back, or side openings. A comfortably fitting waistband is ½–1 in (13–25 mm) larger than the actual waist measurement. Alternative finishes at the waist include facings, and elasticated or drawstring waistbands (see elastic and casings, page 149).

Waistband on garment front

Waistband width – The width of the waistband depends on fashion, style, and personal choice. An average is 1½–2 in (4–5 cm). Whatever the width required, the amount of fabric will be twice the width, plus seam allowances.

Waistband length – The length is determined by size, ease, overlap (if the waistband has an opening), and seam allowances. To the waist size add 1 in (2.5 cm) for comfort ease, 1¼ in (3 cm) for overlap, if required, and 1¼ in (3 cm) for the seam allowance for either end. Therefore for a size 10 (UK size 12), 26½ in (67 cm) waist, you will need a length of waistbanding that is 30 in (75.5 cm).

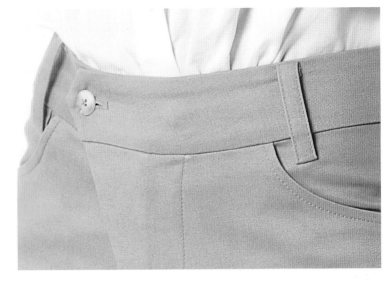

INTERFACING

Waistbands need to be interfaced to provide support and stability. There is a range of waistband interfacings available in different widths, some with perforations for easy folding and seaming, others with stiffeners to prevent waistbands creasing and rolling. For stretch fabrics and knits use a woven sew-in interfacing that has some give in it as well as support.

Always trim interfacing from within the seam allowance to avoid unwanted bulk (the waistband has three layers of fabric: front and back with finished edge. A garment with pleats, darts, and lining can add another 2–3 layers). Trim fusible interfacings to just within the seam allowance before fusing. Trim sew-in interfacings close to the stitching once they have been stitched in place. *Reducing bulk* – As well as trimming interfacing from seam allowances, bulk can be reduced by finishing the raw back edge of the waistband with serging (or use the fabric selvage which doesn't need finishing). An alternative is to interface just half the waistband width with a stiffener such as Petersham.

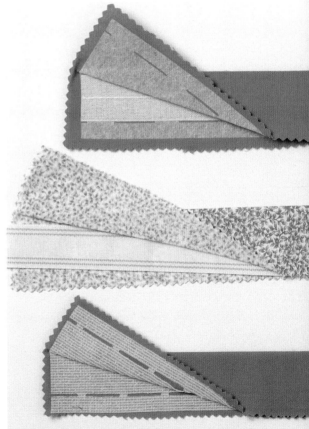

Selection of waistband interfacings

Diagram 1: Pin unfinished long edge to garment

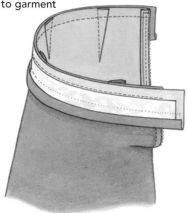

Diagram 2: Slip stitch finished back edge

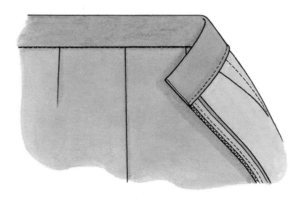

SEWING WAISTBANDS

1. Waistbands are attached to the garment after zipper insertion. Before attaching, finish one long edge (the back edge) by overlocking or turning under by ¼ in (6 mm) and stitching in place.

2. Next, pin the unfinished long edge to the garment, with one end overlapping the garment opening by ⅝ in (1.5 cm) and the other end overlapping by 1¼ in (3 cm) (diagram 1). Evenly distribute the remainder of the waistband along the garment top edge, matching notches and side seams if applicable. Stitch in place then trim and grade the seam allowances by trimming the garment seam allowance to ¼ in (6 mm) and the waistbanding allowance to ⅛ in (3 mm). Press the seam allowances toward the waistband.

3. Fold the waistband in half, right sides together to finish the ends. The finished edge should just sit over the waistband seaming. Taking a ⅝ in (1.5 cm) seam allowance, stitch the overlap from the fold to the seam line. Pivot with the needle down and then stitch along the seam line to the start of the garment. At the other end, simply take a ⅝ in (1.5 cm) seam and stitch

from the fold to the seam line. Trim the seam allowances close to the stitching, snipping the corners at angles and then turn the waistband through and press.

4. Slip stitch the finished back edge of the waistband over the seam allowance on the inside or stitch in the ditch from the right side, pulling the garment and waistband apart as you stitch in the previous seam line and catching the underside of the waistband in place as you stitch (diagram 2).

5. Add a buttonhole to the overlap and buttons to the underneath layer (see buttonholes, page 121) or hand sew a hook and eye fastener in place.

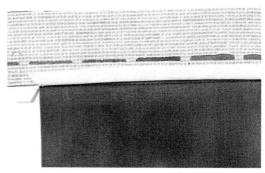

Waistband overlap

COLLARS

Collars consist of at least three layers: upper, interfacing, and under collar. Sometimes there is also a facing. Different collar styles are used for different garments.

Diagram 1: Flat collar

Diagram 2: Rolled collar

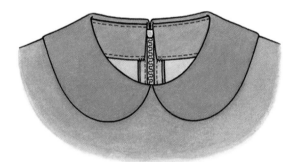

Diagram 3: Standing collar

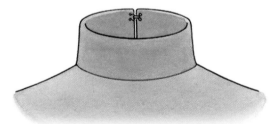

COLLAR TYPES

Flat collar – Lies flat against the neck edge (diagram 1). Used on children's clothing, blouses, jackets, and coats.

Rolled collar – Rises up from neck edge and then rolls down to the garment (diagram 2). The point at which the collar begins to fall is called the roll line. Used on shirts and jackets. Both flat and rolled collars have the upper and under collar cut on the straight of grain from the same pattern piece.

Standing collar – A simple band that rises up from the neck edge (diagram 3). It can be a single width band or a double width band that rolls back on itself. The stand can be straight or shaped. Used on casual tops, blouses, and jackets. A shirt collar has an upright stand with a collar piece that folds down over the stand. The pieces may be separate or cut as one.

Sewing tips

- Select an interfacing that is slightly lighter in weight than the garment fabric and cut on the straight of grain to prevent the collar buckling. Attach interfacing to the upper collar section, trimming the interfacing to just within the seam line to reduce bulk in the seams.
- Make the under collar pattern piece 1/16 in (1–2 mm) smaller than the upper collar section so the seam joining the two pieces rolls slightly to the underside.
- When sewing collar pieces, start in the center and stitch toward either end.
- When stitching pointed collars, reduce the stitch length 1 in (2.5 cm) before and after the corner. Make one stitch diagonally across the corner and then cut triangular shapes from the seam allowances at the corner to reduce bulk (diagram 4).

- Always grade seam allowances – cutting the upper collar to 1/4 in (6 mm) and the under collar to 1/8 in (3 mm). Clip and notch at the curves. Press from both sides before turning through. Use a point turner to ease out the collar point.
- Stay stitch the neck edge of the garment before attaching the collar. Pin the collar, right sides together at the center back, shoulder seams and front, then clip into the seam allowance of the neck edge of the garment to fit the rest of the collar smoothly.

Diagram 4: Pointed collar

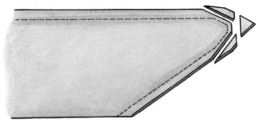

SEWING FLAT AND ROLLED COLLARS

Interface the collar as above. On rolled collars, interface the under collar as well as the upper collar. Add a further strip of interfacing to the roll line on the under collar section to provide additional support for the rise.

Pin and stitch the collar pieces, right sides together around the outer edge, leaving the neck edge open. Trim and finish the seam allowances, clipping and notching the curves. Press the seam allowance toward the under collar and then under stitch them in place to the under collar. Press again before turning right side out. Roll the seam between your finger and thumb to set the seam slightly to the underside. Press in place.

If a flat collar is made up of left and right pieces, slightly overlap at the center front and secure with basting stitches. Prepare the neck edge of the garment.

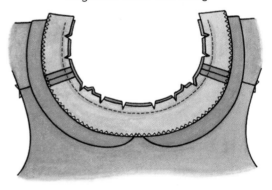

Diagram 5: Collar with facing

Without facing – Finish the neck edge of the upper collar by turning under ¼ in (6 mm) and pressing. Next, pin the under collar only to the garment neck edge, keeping the upper collar free. Stitch in place then trim, clip, and notch the seam allowance. Press toward the collar. Bring the finished upper collar edge over the seam and slip stitch in place.

With facing – Pin and then stitch the complete collar to the neck edge with the under collar close to the garment. Press.

Add the facing, with the outer edge finished, on top of the collar, right sides together. Stitch in place along the neck edge. Trim and grade the seam allowances, clip and notch curves. Note:

the ends of the facing will overlap the garment edge at the back or front opening so they can be turned under and attached to the inside later (diagram 5).

Press the seams open and then press toward the facing. With the facing opened out, under stitch the seam allowances to the facing close to the neck seam line. Turn the facing to the inside and press again. Attach to the garment at the shoulder seams and front or back opening, tucking the raw ends facing inside.

Slip stitching a stand collar to the neck edge

STAND COLLARS

Having interfaced the collar section, fold in half and press to form a fold line. Unfold and tuck under one long edge by ¼ in (6 mm) and finish. Refold the collar along the fold line, right sides together and stitch the short ends. Press the seams open, then toward the underside of the collar.

Turn the collar through to the right side, stitch the remaining long edge to the neck of the garment, keeping the finished edge free. When working with woven fabrics, the garment neck edge needs to be notched and clipped to fit the stand collar. Slip stitch the finished edge to the inside, encasing the seam allowances.

STRETCH KNIT COLLARS

Stretch fabrics are used for stand collars with no openings. Stitch a rectangular band into one piece by stitching short ends together.

Fold the band in half, right sides out, and mark into equal quarters. Turn the garment inside out and pin the collar quarter marks to the center front, center back, and shoulders, with the seam of the collar at the center back. Sew in place with the collar uppermost, using a serger or an over edge stretch stitch, stretching the collar to fit the neck edge between the quarter marks. Remove the pins as you stitch (diagram 6).

Diagram 6: Stretch knit collar

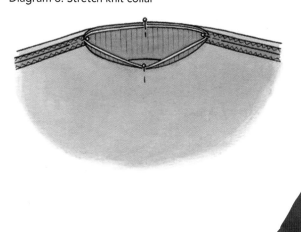

SLEEVES

There are three main sleeve styles. The choice will usually be determined by the garment style. In addition to the style, sleeves can have a variety of hem finishes.

SLEEVE STYLES

Set-in – These fit into a classic armhole. They can have a gathered or pleated sleeve cap. Puff sleeves are also set-in, with exaggerated gathering at the cap. They can be made of one or two pieces and may have elbow shaping created with small darts or ease stitching. Shirt sleeves, which have a smaller sleeve cap, can be attached to the garment back or front prior to the sleeve and side seams being stitched.

Raglan – These sleeves have a diagonal seam from the inner neck to the underarm. To produce a closer fit at the top of the sleeve, a dart is inserted from the neck edge. A two-piece raglan sleeve will be joined to the front and back of the garment prior to the sleeve sections being joined.

Diagram 1: Set-in (l), raglan (r), and kimono (bottom) sleeves

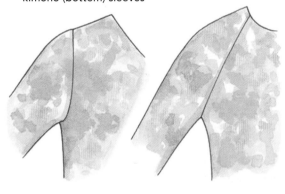

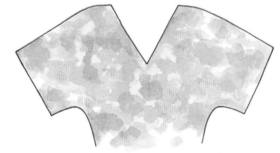

Kimono – These sleeves are cut as one with the front and back of the garment. They can be capped or long, depending on style. Drop shoulder sleeves are a variation of the kimono style, where an additional rectangular sleeve is attached to the garment back or front before the underarm sleeve and side seams are sewn (diagram 1).

SEWING TIPS

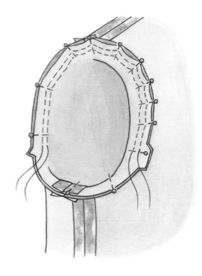

Diagram 2: Fitting the sleeve

- Sleeve patterns tend to have a double notch at the back and a single notch at the front which will match double or single notches on the back and front of the garment.
- Set-in sleeves may need ease stitching around the sleeve cap to help fit them into the armhole. Stitch two rows, with a slightly longer stitch length, just inside the seam allowance.
- Pin the sleeve in position, matching the top of the sleeve cap, notches, and underarm seam. Pull up the ease stitching using the bobbin thread until the sleeve fits (diagram 2).
- Start stitching from the underarm seam with the sleeve uppermost.
- Trim the seam allowances and finish with overcast or zigzag stitch.

HEMMING SLEEVES

Apart from cuffs and plackets (see cuffs, page 113), sleeves can be finished with a simple double hem, with self-casing, and a ruffle or bias binding (ideal for sheer fabrics where the inside of the hem is visible).

Self-hem – On light- or medium-weight fabrics, turn a double hem by turning under ⅜ in (1 cm) twice, with the raw edge touching the first fold. Top stitch in place, working from the right side. On heavyweight fabrics, finish the hem edge with zigzag or overlock stitch and then turn up the hem allowance. Either top stitch from the right side or slip stitch the inside to the garment by hand.

Gathered with self-casing – This is formed by folding the hem allowance to the inside and stitching along both edges (raw and fold) to form a casing. Leave a gap in the upper row of stitching into which the elastic can be inserted. Insert the elastic and sew the ends together securely before closing the gap with slip stitching. Alternatively, gather the end of the sleeve with a long gathering stitch and attach a separate cuff as detailed on pages 113–15 (diagram 3).

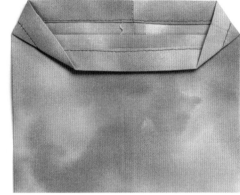

Double hemmed sleeve with top stitching

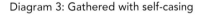
Diagram 3: Gathered with self-casing

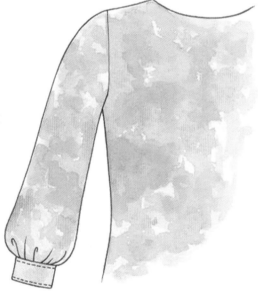

HELPFUL HINT:
On thick, bulky fabrics, trim the seam allowance of the underarm seam within the hem allowance area to reduce bulk prior to turning up the hem.

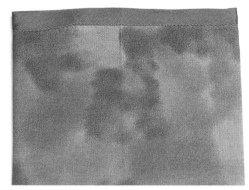

Bias bound sleeve

Diagram 4: Bias binding

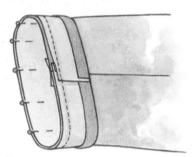

Ruffle – A ruffle adds extra length to the sleeve in order to create a self-faced casing. The amount to add depends on the required depth of the ruffle – allow 5–6 in (13–15 cm) for a 3–4 in (8–10 cm) ruffle, plus casing. Finish the raw edge of the sleeve, turn up at the hem length and then stitch close to the finished edge and then again approximately 1 in (2.5 cm) away from the first row to form a casing. Leave a gap in the first row into which the elastic can be inserted.

Bias binding – Open out the bias binding along one long edge and then pin to the sleeve edge, right sides together. Turn the raw end closest to the garment over to finish the raw edge. Overlap the ends and machine stitch along the preformed foldline of the bias binding (diagram 4). Trim the seam allowances and turn the binding to the inside, encasing the raw edges. Stitch in the ditch from the right side, catching the bias trim in place or slip stitch in place by hand.

CUFFS

Cuffs can be simple bands, have plackets, a continuous lap, a hemmed opening, or can be cut from contrasting fabric such as fur or knit rib.

SIMPLE CUFFS

Sleeve cuffs are generally formed from a top layer, interfacing, and under layer or facing. The top and facing are often cut as one piece and folded in half, with the top half interfaced. Cuffs, also known as turn-ups on trousers or short sleeves, are made from an extended hem edge that is shaped to turn up easily.

This method creates a cuff from one piece of fabric, folded to form a cuff and facing.

1. Cut a rectangle that is wrist circumference, plus 3 in (8 cm) for wearing ease and seam allowances, by approximately 6¼ in (16 cm) wide. Interface half the width, excluding the seam allowance, and then finish the other long edge (diagram 1).
2. With right sides together, fold the cuff in two lengthwise, so the finished edge overlaps the raw edge by ⅝ in (1.5 cm). Stitch the side seams, taking a ⅝ in (1.5 cm) seam allowance. Trim, cutting the corners at angles and turn through, using a point turner to push the corners out neatly.

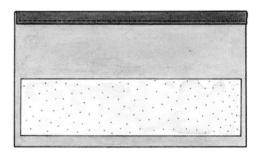

Simple cuff band attached to sleeve

Diagram 1: Cuff from 1 piece of fabric

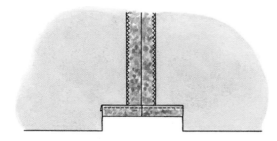

Cuff with hemmed opening

HEMMED-OPENING CUFFS

Before adding the cuff, make a small hem opening at the sleeve hem by reinforcing the stitching 1½ in (3 cm) either side of the underarm seam, stitching along the seam line. Clip up from the hem edge to the stitching at either end, taking care not to cut the stitching, then turn the flap up and the raw edge under again. Stitch in place (diagram 2).

Diagram 2: Hemmed-opening cuff

SEAM-OPENING CUFF

An alternative to the continuous lap cuff, this is a simple method of creating a wider cuff opening. Stitch the sleeve seam to within 3 in (8 cm) of the end and press the seam allowance open. Finish the raw edges to the end of the seam stitching. Snip into the seam allowance at right angles and then turn the remaining seam allowance under to hem. Machine stitch in place down both sides of the opening and across the top (diagram 3).

Diagram 3: Seam-opening cuff

CONTINUOUS-LAP CUFF

This is created in the sleeve fabric, approximately 4–5 in (10–13 cm) from the sleeve seam and is applied prior to stitching the seam. It is the most widely used opening, although it is not recommended on bulky fabrics.

1. Cut a bias strip of self-fabric 1½ in (3 cm) wide and 6 in (15 cm) long. Turn one long edge to the wrong side and press.
2. Mark an upturned V shape, 3 in (8 cm) long and 1½ in (3 cm) wide at the sleeve edge. Stitch the V, reducing the stitch length just before and after the point then cut up the center of the V almost to the stitching at the point. Spread open the slashed edge and then pin, right sides together, the raw edge of the bias binding to the slash. Machine stitch in place. Turn the finished binding edge to the inside, encasing the raw edges and slip stitch in place (diagram 4).
3. Refold the lapped edges to bring the hem edge back in line, with the front part of the lap to the inside. Stitch the underarm seam.

ATTACHING CUFFS

Pin then stitch the raw edge of the prepared cuff to the sleeve edge, right sides together, matching the openings. Trim and grade the seam allowances and press toward the cuff. Fold the facing to the inside, covering the seam allowances, and slip stitch in place.

Alternative cuff finishes also include vents (for tailored jackets) and plackets (used for men's shirts). Plackets are made from separate fabric pieces that are contrasting or of the same fabric and are attached to the sleeve opening (diagram 5).

Continuous-lap cuff

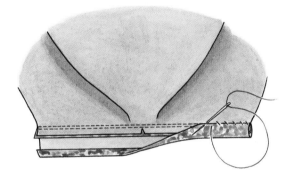

Diagram 4: Continuous-lap cuff

Diagram 5: Placket

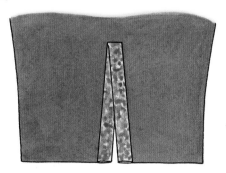

ZIPPERS

Zippers can be inserted in two main ways – centered or lapped. In addition there are different types of zippers: some are used as decorative detailing, while invisible zippers are hidden within the seams of a garment to be virtually invisible.

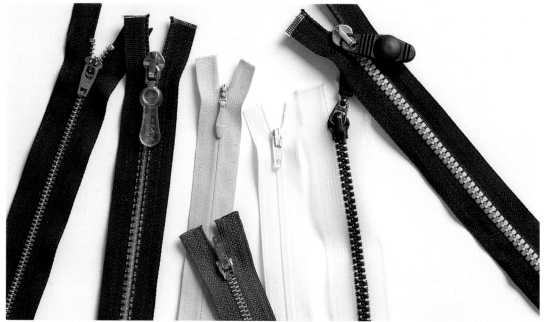

Selection of zippers

ZIPPER TYPES

Today these come not only with nylon or metal teeth, but also with decorative teeth such as clear, crystal, silver, and coated. Lightweight zippers have nylon zipper tapes and teeth. Heavier metal zippers have cotton tapes. Zippers also come in a number of lengths and colors to suit most applications – including continuous (you cut to the length required) and double-ended.

Centered zippers – These are stitched with equal edges that meet in the center of the zipper teeth. The stitching shows from the right-hand side of the garment. Used for dresses, front closure on jackets, etc., and on soft furnishings

Centered zipper in place

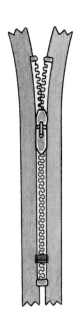

Lapped zippers – These are stitched so that one side of the zipper is attached to the edge of the folded-under seam allowance, the other to the seam line so that when it is closed, the fabric laps over. Only one side of the stitching shows from the outside. Used on trousers and skirts. A fly front zipper is similar, with a wider lap.

GENERAL SEWING TIPS

- Finish the seam allowance of seams that will have a zipper prior to zipper insertion.
- Position the zipper so that there is room for facings, waistbands, collars, etc.
- If adding a zipper to lightweight or stretchy fabrics, add stay tape or lightweight interfacing to the seam allowance of the area in which the zipper is to be inserted to improve stability.
- Use a special zipper foot on the sewing machine to allow stitching close to the teeth (invisible zippers need a special invisible zipper foot).

CENTERED ZIPPER

1. Pin the seam, right sides together, and position the closed zipper in place. Mark the base of the zipper. Remove and baste the seam from the top to the mark, then change to a regular stitch length to finish the seam from the mark to the hem (diagram 1). Press the seam allowance open.

2. Replace the zipper, right side down, with the teeth in the center of the basted seam line. Baste the zipper tape in place on both sides, basting through the seam allowance and the main fabric.

Diagram 1: Centered zipper

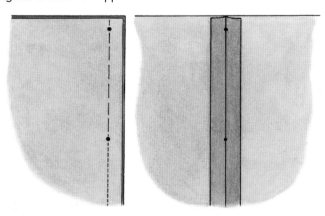

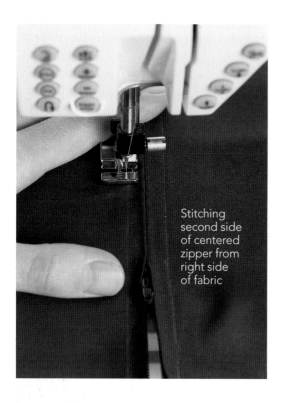

Stitching second side of centered zipper from right side of fabric

3. Working from the right side and using a zipper foot, machine stitch from the bottom of the zipper at the seam, stitch a few stitches then pivot and stitch up the side to the top. Repeat for the other side, again starting at the center bottom of the zipper. Remove the basting.

HELPFUL HINT:
As you get close to the zipper pull, stop stitching, with the needle down and the foot raised. Open the zipper, working the pull past the presser foot. Finish stitching the side.

LAPPED ZIPPER

1. Mark the zipper position, baste, and stitch the seam as for the centered zipper.
2. Unzip the zipper and with right side down, place on the left seam allowance so the teeth are on the seam line. Pin and baste to the seam allowance only, basting down the center of the zipper tape (diagram 2).
3. Close the zipper, then turn it face up, creating a fold in the seam allowance along the teeth edge. Machine stitch as close to the teeth as possible with a zipper foot, starting at the zipper bottom (diagram 3). Clip the seam allowance below the zipper end.
4. Working from the right side of the garment, smooth flat, checking the zipper is even and flat also. Baste the right-hand zipper tape through all thicknesses across the bottom and up the side, approximately ½ in (13 mm) from the seam line. Machine stitch along the basting stitching, again working from bottom to top.

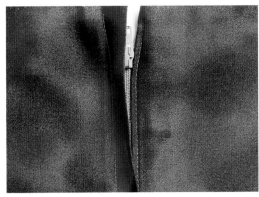

Lapped zipper

Stitching a lapped zipper from the right side of the garment

Diagram 2: Pin and baste to seam allowance

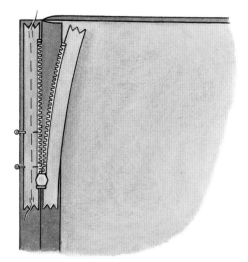

Diagram 3: Machine stitch the closed zipper

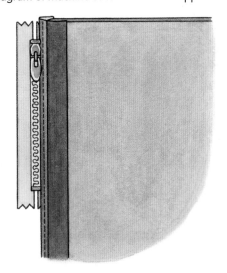

OPEN ENDED/SEPARATING ZIPPER

Zippers that open at both ends can be inserted using the centered or lapped zipper methods. They are often made from heavier-weight fabric and metal teeth, and are used on sportswear, vests, and jackets. Insert zippers before adding front facings and hemming. For easy and quick insertion, separate the zipper and work with each half separately before rejoining.

INVISIBLE ZIPPERS

The invisible zipper is a special type of zipper that has no coils showing on the right side of the zipper tape and thus is virtually invisible from the right side of garment. This zipper is inserted into a seam prior to the seam being constructed. In order to be properly stitched in place, you need to use an invisible zipper presser foot.

1. Open the zipper and press the coils of the zipper open with an iron to keep them away from the zipper tape.
2. On the left-hand garment section, place the right side of the zipper onto the right side of the fabric. Position the zipper so that the coils align with the stitching line ⅝ in (1.5 cm) from the cut edge. Baste in place (diagram 4).
3. Keeping the zipper open and using an invisible zipper foot, machine stitch the zipper in place so that the coils feed through the left-hand groove in the foot. Stop when the machine foot touches the puller on the zipper and fix the machine stitch.
4. Close the zipper. Position the right-hand side of the garment over the left-hand side of the garment, aligning the cut edges. Pin the zipper in position on the right-hand garment section. Open the zipper again and baste in place.
5. Machine stitch in place, this time with the coils feeding through the right-hand groove in the machine foot.
6. To complete the seam below the zipper, close the zipper and pin the remainder of the seam together. Using a regular zipper foot, stitch the seam, starting as close to the end of the zipper as possible (pull the end of the zipper tape away from the seam at the start). Press the seam allowance open.
7. Secure the last 2 in (5 cm) of the zipper tape to the seam allowance.

Invisible zipper

Diagram 4: Baste invisible zipper in place

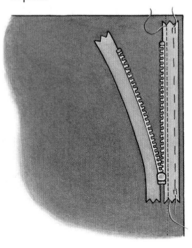

BUTTONHOLES

When the correct combination of fabric, stabilizer or interfacing, thread, and sharp needle are used, beautiful buttonholes are easily achieved on today's modern sewing machines, whether in one, three, or more steps.

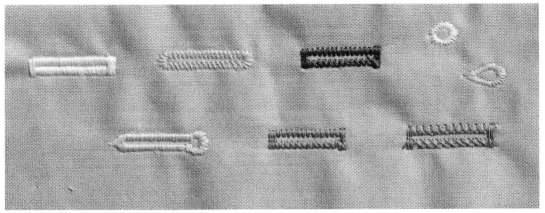

Selection of buttonholes

BASIC BUTTONHOLES

A basic buttonhole comprises a bar tack at either end and two sides which are closely satin stitched. Depending on your sewing machine, this might be stitched in one operation (one step) or require dials or buttons to be turned after each step – first side, bar tack, second side, final bar tack. Check your user's manual to determine the buttonhole functions you have.

General sewing tips

- Interface or stabilize the buttonhole area with fusible interfacing or tearaway stabilizer.
- Use an all-purpose thread in both the bobbin and as the top thread.
- As the buttonhole comprises dense, close stitching, penetrating at least three or more layers, use a new sharp needle so that it can pierce three or more layers of fabric easily.

- Determine the buttonhole size by measuring the button circumference. Halve the measurement and add ⅛ in (3 mm). Unusually shaped or domed buttons may require larger buttonholes.
- Always test buttonholes on fabric scraps, with the same fabric layers and interfacing prior to stitching on the garment.
- Once stitched, feed the thread tails back through the stitching before cutting them off.

Stabilizing the buttonhole area

Buttonholes can be successfully stitched in any fabric, from lightweight sheers to heavyweight or stretch knits. To achieve a neat buttonhole, the fabric needs to be stabilized with interfacing or stabilizer to prevent the concentrated stitching puckering the fabric if it is lightweight, or stretching if it is a knit fabric. Most areas that

HELPFUL HINT:
Special-purpose buttonhole thread can be used for heavyweight garments which require very strong buttonholes.

require buttonholes are usually already interfaced – facings, waistbands, front openings, etc. However, if they are not, add a small square of tearaway stabilizer behind the area to be stitched to provide the stability needed. It will also help the buttonhole retain shape when in use. If stitching very lightweight chiffons, add a further layer of water-soluble or tearaway stabilizer to help prevent the fine fabric being pulled down into the feed dogs (see interfacings and stabilizers, page 39).

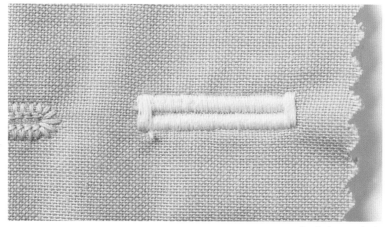

Basic buttonhole

Marking the buttonhole positions

Buttonholes should be positioned at least ¾ in (2 cm) from the garment edge. On average, buttons should be placed approximately 2–3 in (5–8 cm) apart on garments and 4–5 in (10–13 cm) apart on soft furnishings. On lightweight fabrics, position them slightly closer.

Diagram 1: Mark buttonhole positions

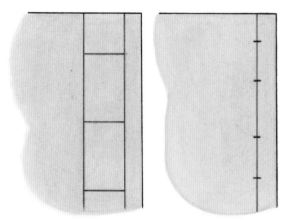

Mark the buttonhole placement with chalk lines or basting stitches. For horizontal buttons, draw two parallel lines the buttonhole size apart, down the length to be buttoned. Draw the buttonhole positions. For vertical buttons, draw a vertical line from top to bottom of the buttonhole placement and then mark the buttonhole size with tiny horizontal lines, spacing them evenly down the placement line. Note: Commercial patterns will have buttonhole placement marks on the tissue; transfer these marks to the fabric (diagram 1).

Opening the buttonhole

To open a buttonhole, place a pin at one end close to the inner edge of the bar tack and, starting from other end, push a seam ripper (quick unpick) toward the pin and between the side stitching.

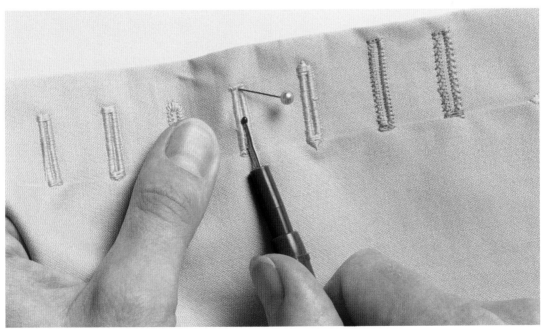

Opening a buttonhole

BOUND BUTTONHOLES

These designer-style buttonholes have lips on either side of the opening. They are quite awkward to do, so are best avoided on fabrics that fray easily.

1. Cut a rectangle of fabric 2 in (5 cm) longer than the buttonhole and baste to the right side of the garment, centered over the buttonhole position. (To help center accurately, fold a rectangle in half and crease the fold. Open out and place the crease over the buttonhole.)

2. Mark the buttonhole position plus a rectangle around the buttonhole, ⅛ in (3 mm) away from the marked line on either side.

3. Machine stitch the rectangle, counting the number of stitches taken on the short ends to ensure both are the same (diagram 2).

4. Starting at the center and using a small pair of sharp scissors, cut the buttonhole down the length and then diagonally toward the corners of the rectangle, taking care not to cut the stitching.

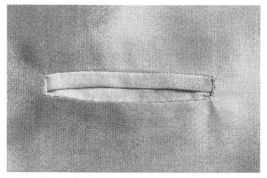

Bound buttonhole

Diagram 2: Machine stitch the rectangle

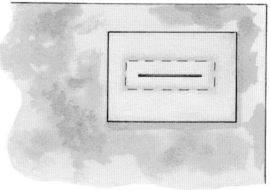

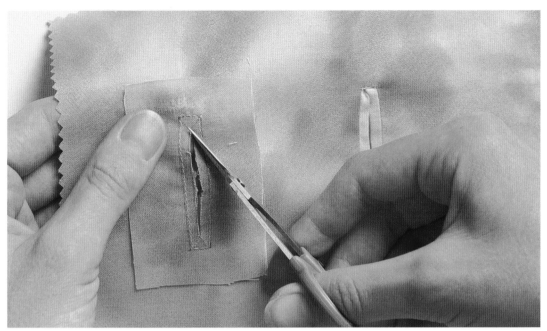

Cutting into the corners of the buttonhole

Diagram 3: Stitch through all layers of patch

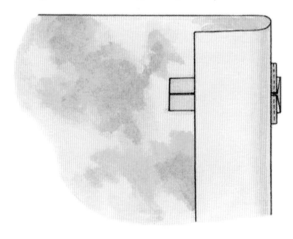

5. Push the patch through the buttonhole, rolling the seam so it is on the edge of the buttonhole. Press.

6. Form the buttonhole lips by folding the long edges over the opening, with the folded edges meeting at the center of the buttonhole. Check that the lips are even from the right side and then baste to hold in place.

7. Working from the right side of the garment, fold the garment back along the side of the buttonhole, exposing the ends of the patch. Stitch across, through all layers of the patch, close to the garment fold. Repeat at the other end of buttonhole (diagram 3).

8. Do the same at the top and bottom of the buttonhole – fold the garment back to expose the patch and stitch inside the original stitching line. Open out the garment and press with a press cloth.

FASTENINGS

These include buttons, button loops, hooks and eyes, hook and loop, and snap fasteners. Zippers and buttonholes are covered in separate chapters.

BUTTONS

Buttons come in many shapes and sizes but with just two types of sewing attachment – sew-through holes or a shank. Shanked buttons are best used on thicker fabrics and multi-layers. Sew-through buttons are ideal for lightweight garments.

Selection of buttons

General sewing tips

- Position buttons ⅛ in (3 mm) in from the outer edge of the horizontal buttonhole and ⅛ in (3 mm) from the top of the vertical buttonhole.
- Stitch with a double strand of all-purpose thread.
- When attaching sew-through buttons, place a small stick (match or cocktail) over the button and take stitches over the stick, taking 3–4 stitches through each hole. Remove the stick and pull the button up so the excess thread is between the button base and the fabric. With the needle between the button and the fabric, wind the thread around the stitching to form a small thread shank (diagram 1). Take the needle to the reverse of the fabric and tie off.

Diagram 1: Thread shank for sew-through button

Self-covered buttons

Self-covered buttons

Ideal when a perfect match is desired, or when suitable buttons are unavailable, self-covered buttons come in various sizes and in plastic and metal. Instructions to cover are included in the packaging.

- If you are using lightweight fabric, cover metal buttons with lightweight interfacing or use a double layer of fabric.
- Avoid bulky fabrics or loosely woven fabrics which will be hard to gather and clip in the button back. Instead, cover with similarly colored medium-weight fabric.

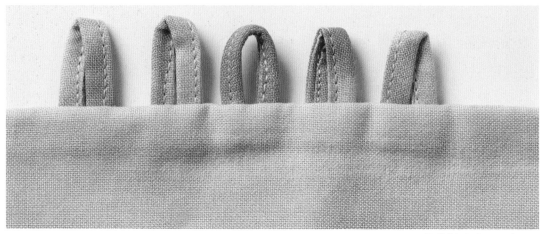

Self-fabric button loops

Button loops

Used instead of buttonholes, button loops are often a decorative detail on jackets and bridal dresses and are combined with round or unusual-shaped buttons which might be difficult to slip through buttonholes. Loops can be made from strips of bias-cut fabric, from braid, or purchased as ready-made loops on a tape.

Looped tape – Sandwich the tape between the main fabric and the facing, with the tape edge matching the garment edge and the loops to the inside. Stitch through all thicknesses close to the loops (diagram 2). When turned through, the loops will protrude from the fabric edge.

Self-fabric button loops – Cut a bias strip approximately ¾ in (2 cm) wide by the length needed. Cut a length of string 5 in (13 cm) longer than fabric (this is used to help turn the bias strip through to the right side). Fold the fabric in half, right sides together, with the string inside the fold. Stitch across one end, catching the string end in the stitching and taking a ⅜ in (1 cm) seam. Without trimming the seam allowances (which will help fill out the tube), pull free the string end to pull the fabric through. Cut off the string.

Measure the buttons and then cut the fabric tube into suitable lengths, remembering to allow ⅝ in (1.5 cm) at either end for seam allowances. Pin the loops in position to the right side of the garment edge, with loops facing in and raw edges matching. Hand baste in position before adding facing as for the looped tape.

Diagram 2: Looped tape

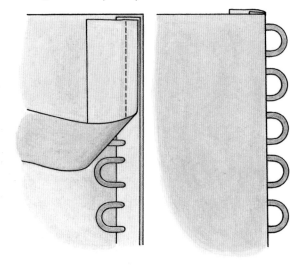

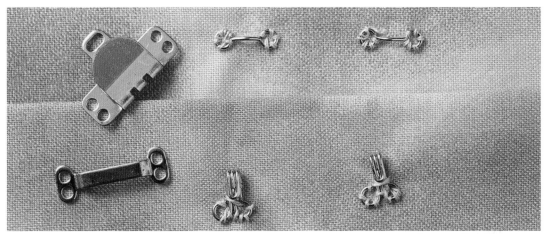

HOOKS AND EYES

Ranging in size and weight, these two-piece fasteners have a hook on one piece and an eye (loop) on the other. They can be used as an additional fastener at the top of zippers or alone. Use double thread or buttonhole twist thread to sew in place.

SNAPS

Snaps, or poppers, are another fastener used on areas that will not take much strain. Ideal for children's clothing, they are easily pushed or "snapped" together to fasten. Like hooks and eyes, they come in two parts, a ball and a socket. Place the ball section on the under lap of the garment and the socket on the overlap. Stitch with double thread.

Snaps or poppers and snap tape

HELPFUL HINT:
Prevent the stitching showing on the right side of the garment by just picking up one or two fibers from the inside of the main fabric when stitching the socket in place. Stitch two to three times through each hole on the socket.

In addition to individual snap fasteners, snap tape is available on which the snaps are evenly spaced. These are ideal for bed linen and baby's clothing. Separate the tape sections and stitch one side to one fabric edge, stitching along both long edges of the tape. Stitch the corresponding tape in position on the matching fabric, ensuring the snaps are lined up.

HOOK AND LOOP FASTENER (VELCRO)

Again, a two-part fastener, this is made up of two strips of nylon, one with tiny hooks and the other with a fluffy looped side. When placed together the hooks grab the loops and hold firm. Available in different widths and colors, some hook and loop fasteners are fusible, others are sew-in or have one strip to sew in and the other fusible – useful when attaching curtains to wooden battens, etc. Also now available are single strip hook and loop tapes, which have both hooks and loops on the same strip.

Hook and loop fastener attached to fabric

TUCKS AND PLEATS

Tucks and pleats are formed by folding fabric back on itself to take in excess fabric, provide shaping, or simply to create a design detail. Because they are created by fabric folds, more fabric is required than normal. How much extra is required will depend on the number and size of the pleats. Tucks are generally smaller than pleats and are sewn in place along the folded edge, while pleats tend to be sewn at the top or part of the way down only.

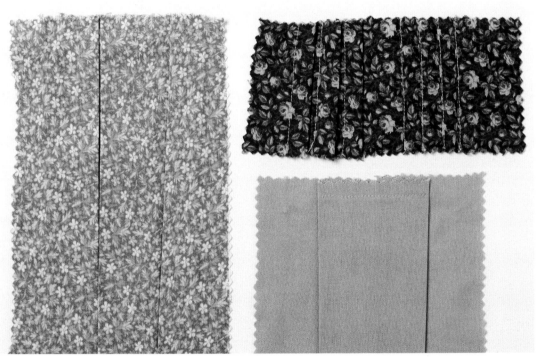

Selection of tucks and pleats

TUCKS

Not only do tucks add decorative detail, they can also be used to help with fit. It is important to measure and sew tucks accurately to ensure the correct amount of fabric is tucked – a difference of just ⅛ in (3 mm) per tuck could affect the fit. For example, eight tucks, each out by ⅛ in (3 mm), equals an overall difference of 1 in (2.5 cm).

Tucks are taken along the straight grain, parallel with the selvages or fabric threads. Press vertical tucks away from the center front or back and horizontal tucks downward. There are three main types of tuck: pin, corded, or wide.

Pin tuck – Often used on blouses, pin tucks are very narrow. Used on fine lightweight fabrics.

Corded – Formed by laying a cord within the fold of the fabric, resulting in a small, raised tuck.

Wide tuck – A wider version of a pin tuck and similar to a pleat.

General sewing tips

- For tucks used as a decorative feature, transfer the markings or fold points to the right side of the garment. If the tucks are folded and stitched inside the garment, transfer the markings to the wrong side.

- Unless you are using a commercial pattern (which includes placement marks), make a cardboard template with notches to indicate the tuck depth and the gap between the folds. Note there will be a fold line and a stitching line. With the template placed on the fabric, mark the tuck stitching line and the fold line by cutting tiny notches in the seam allowance or marking with a chalk pencil or tailor's tack. Mark at either end of the tuck to ensure accurate folding. Fold the fabric along the fold line and lap it to the stitching line. Press in place (diagram 1).

Diagram 1: Cardboard template for tucks

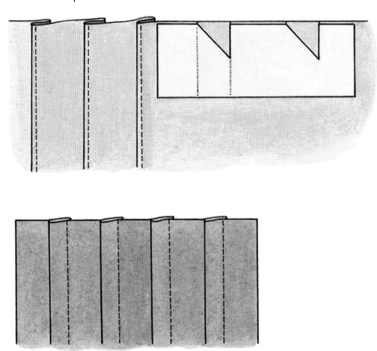

- For decorative tucks on the right side, stitch close to the fold on the inside. For tucks on the inside, stitch close to the fold on the right side.
- Pin tucks are usually approximately ⅜ in (1 cm). Wide tucks can be ¼–½ in (6–13 mm).
- For corded tucks, fold the tuck as before and add the cord within the fold on the wrong side of the garment. Working from the right side with a zipper or cording foot, stitch through both fabric layers as close to the cord as possible (diagram 2).

Diagram 2: Corded tucks

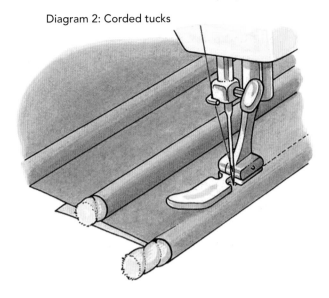

Diagram 3: Tuck the fabric first

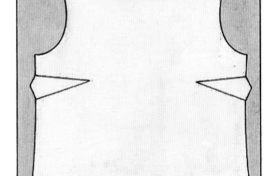

HELPFUL HINT:
If you are adding tucks to a garment, first tuck the fabric, then cut out the pattern to ensure enough fabric is allowed for each pattern piece and to position tucks where desired (diagram 3).

Diagram 4: Fold and placement lines

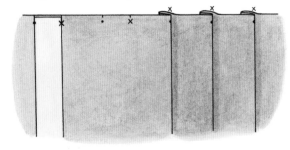

Diagram 5: Stitch to keep pleats in place

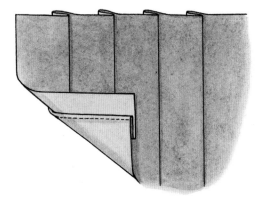

HELPFUL HINT:
Use fusible waist-band interfacing on the wrong side for crisp, even pleats.

Pleat with waistband interfacing inside

PLEATS

As with tucks, there are three main pleat variations:

Knife pleats – These are straight pleats, all facing the same direction, lapping right over left.

Box pleats – Made from two pleats, turned away from each other to form a panel.

Inverted pleats – Two straight pleats turned toward each other to form a V opening. Kick pleats are a variation of the inverted pleat and may have the underlay section cut from a contrast fabric to add design detail.

General sewing tips

- As with tucks, unless you are using a commercial pattern, make a template from stiff card, cut to the width of the finished pleat – i.e., ¾ in (2 cm) wide. Mark the "placement line" on one edge and "fold line" on the other. Use the template to transfer the markings to the fabric, using a different mark for fold and placement lines for easy identification (diagram 4). For unpressed pleats, mark down lines just 2–4 in (5–10 cm) from the top edge. For crisp, pressed pleats, mark the whole pleat length.
- Keeping the upper edges even, fold the pleat along the fold line to meet the placement line. Pin and baste in place along the top edge.
- Hem the garment before forming the pleats, if possible.
- Always press with a press cloth to avoid leaving fold imprints on the fabric.
- To keep pleats in place, working from the wrong side, machine stitch close to the inner fold, particularly in the hem area (diagram 5).

LININGS AND INTERLININGS

Many garments are lined to give extra body and to help them hang properly. Linings will also cover seams, interfacings, etc. They can be made from any lightweight fabric, although most are constructed from lining fabric, which is usually nylon or silk. They can be in a matching color or a striking contrast color, but do need to be compatible with the main fabric in terms of laundering.

HELPFUL HINT:
To allow for wearing ease, reduce the dart size in the back of the jacket lining and then take a pleat at the center of the neck edge to provide the extra fullness.

LOOSE LININGS

Loose linings use the same pattern pieces as the garment, excluding facings, waistbands, collars, and cuffs. They are stitched together in the same manner as the garment before being attached to the garment at the neck, waist, etc., before facings are applied. Leave openings for zippers about 1 in (2.5 cm) longer than the zipper placement on the garment.

Having sewn both lining and main garment up to the point of the facings, with wrong sides together, pin the lining to the garment at the neck and front opening on jackets, at the neck and armholes on dresses, and at the waist on skirts or trousers. Match seams, darts, notches, and raw edges. Baste, then machine stitch along the edges pinned together.

Diagram 1: Lining with a zipper

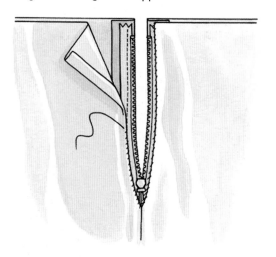

Zippers

When lining a garment with a zipper, at the zipper area, turn the raw edge of the lining under and slip stitch to the zipper tape (diagram 1).

Necklines and armholes

Necklines and armholes are then finished with facings (see facings and bands, page 92) so that when turned to the inside they encase the raw edges (diagram 2). Finish the waist edge with facing or waistbands (see waistbands, page 102).

Hems

Turn the lining hem up so that the fold sits just over the stitched hem edge of the garment. Keeping the garment free, tuck the raw edge of the lining to the inside and then machine stitch the hem (diagram 3).

Diagram 2: Neckline finished with facing

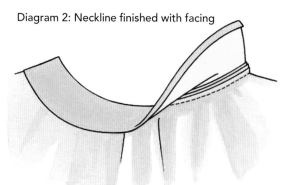

Diagram 3: Machine stitch the hem

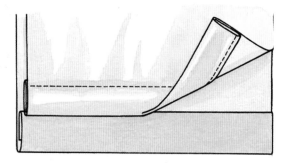

INTERLININGS

Interlinings, also known as underlinings, are another layer, sandwiched between the main fabric and the lining. Interlinings are often sewn with the main fabric as one, adding stability and body to the main fabric. They are cut from the same pattern pieces as the main fabric, excluding facings, collars, and cuffs. Transfer the pattern markings to the right side of the interlining and then place the interlining to the fabric, wrong sides together. Baste the layers together around the edges and through the darts, etc. Then construct the garment in the usual way, treating the two layers as one.

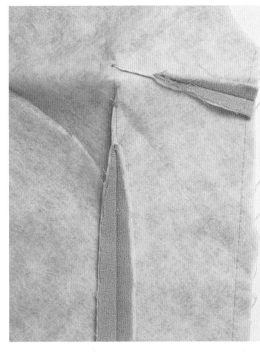

GATHERS AND RUFFLES

Fabric is gathered to reduce the length to fit on to a straight edge. Ruffles are gathered pieces of fabric added as a decorative detail. They can be wide or narrow, made from the same or contrasting fabric.

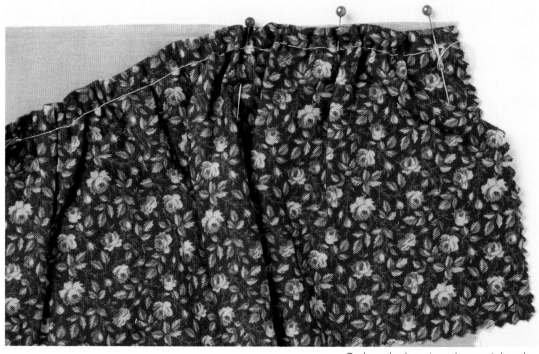

Gathered edge pinned to straight edge

GATHERS

1. Use a long basting stitch (the longest stitch available on your sewing machine). Use a contrasting color thread both in the bobbin and on top so the stitches can easily be removed later.

2. Leave long thread tails at each end of the stitching and stitch within the seam allowance. Pull up using the bobbin thread, adjusting the gathers evenly along the length as you go. If gathering a long edge, divide the length in half and stitch and gather each half at a time. When sewing medium- to heavyweight fabrics,

stitch two rows of gathering stitch and pull up both together.

3. Once fully gathered to fit the straight edge, tie off the tails to keep the fabric gathered. Pin with right sides together and machine stitch with the gathered fabric uppermost.

4. Press carefully to avoid crushing the fabric gathers.

Diagram 1: Use a cord to create gathers

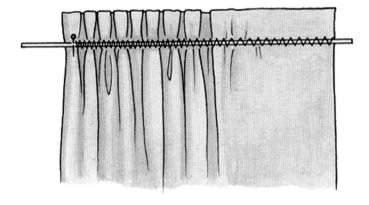

RUFFLES

1. To determine the ruffle length, measure the straight edge onto which the ruffle is to be attached. For lightweight fabrics multiply by three. For heavyweight fabrics multiply by one and a half to two.

2. Ruffle depth depends on personal preference, however on children's clothing 1–3 in (2.5–8 cm) works well, and on soft furnishings and heavyweight fabric a deeper ruffle of 6–8 in (15–20 cm) is more suitable.

3. Hem ruffle strips before gathering. On lightweight fabrics and stretch fabrics use a rolled or lettuce edge hem (see hemming, page 86). Alternatively, take a double hem by folding up the hem allowance and tucking the raw edge under again to meet the first fold. Machine stitch in place.

4. If the ruffle is to be added on top of the main fabric and thus both long edges will be visible, hem both before gathering. Hem the top edge with a ⅝ in (1.5 cm) top stitch. Once gathered, pin in position, with the wrong side of the ruffle to the right side of the fabric. Stitch in place, stitching over the previous top stitching (diagram 2).

Diagram 2: Ruffle on top of main fabric

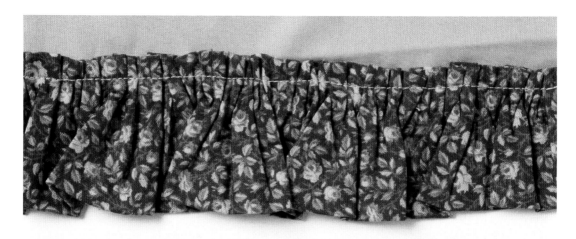

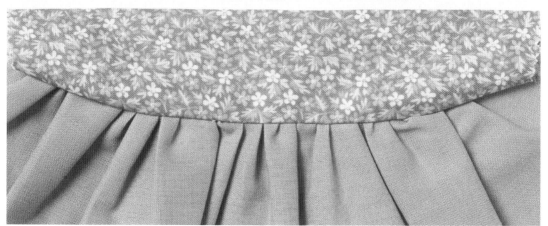

Ruffle examples

5. When adding a ruffle to a hemline, first reduce the length of the skirt or dress by the depth of ruffle (to avoid lengthening the garment). Do this by cutting off the ruffle depth less ⅝ in (1.5 cm) for the seam allowance. Turn up the raw edge of the garment by the seam allowance and press. Pin the right side of the ruffle to the underside of the garment, matching the raw edge of the ruffle with the turned up edge of the garment. Working from the right side, top stitch in place, stitching close to the garment fold and catching the ruffle in place as you stitch (diagram 3).

Diagram 3: Top stitch the ruffle in place

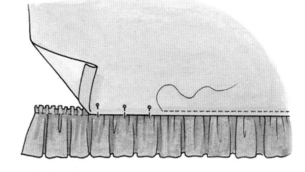

FANCY EDGES

There are many ways to finish edges other than by simply finishing them. These include bias binding and piping in matching or contrasting colors, lace edging, and fringe.

Bias binding being made with a bias tape maker

BIAS BINDING

Bias binding is made from strips of fabric cut on the bias so that it can curve around corners without puckering, and is folded in half with the long edges tucked in again. One edge is slightly wider than the other (diagram 1). It is used to cover raw edges and provide a decorative trim at the same time. It works well on unlined garments such as edge-to-edge jackets or vests, children's clothes and craft projects, as well as providing a great finish for necklines and armholes. Foldover braid is similar to bias binding, without the tucked under edges. It is used in the same way.

Diagram 1: Bias binding

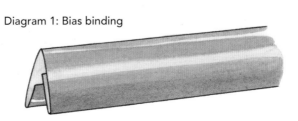

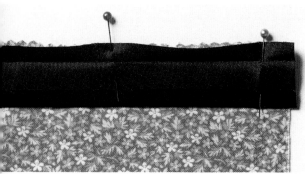

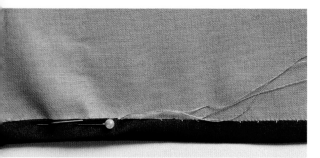

Bias binding being stitched to the fabric edge

Bias bound fabric edge

Bias binding can be made in self-fabrics using a bias tape maker (available in various widths) or purchased ready-made, again in different widths and fabric finishes. The choice of binding width depends on the style and fabric to be bound. Lightweight fabrics can be bound with narrow bias binding, while heavyweight fabrics need wider bindings to accommodate the bulk of the seam allowances.

If available for your sewing machine, use a bias binding foot through which the tape is fed and wrapped around the fabric edge as you sew. However, it is simple to add the tape without the foot as follows:

1. Open the narrowest edge along the side of the bias tape and pin to the garment edge, right sides together. Stitch in place along the crease of the opened edge.
2. Trim the seam allowance and then fold the tape over to the reverse of the work, encasing the raw edges. Slip stitch in place. Alternatively, stitch in the ditch from the right side, gently pulling the binding and fabric apart to stitch within the previous seam and catching the underside of the bias binding in place.

Joining ends

• To join ends, for instance on a neck or armhole, first pin the binding to the edge as before, starting at the center back or back of armhole. Turn the raw edge of the start of the binding over and pin to hold. Lap the other end over the top of the folded end. Stitch in place (diagram 2). Once the binding is turned to the inside of the garment, the finished edge will be on the outside.

Diagram 2: Joining ends

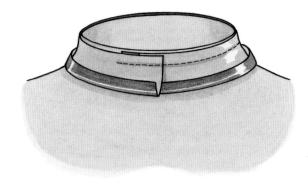

Handling corners

- *Outer corners* – Stitch the binding as before, stopping ⅝ in (1.5 cm) from the corner. Fold the binding away from the corner at right angles to make a diagonal fold, pin in place. Then refold along the next edge and start stitching again from where you finished (⅝ in/1.5 cm from the raw edges) (diagram 3).

  Fold the binding to the underside as before. A miter will automatically form on the right side. On the inside, fold the corner into a neat miter and slip stitch in place. Slip stitch the rest of the binding as before.

- *Inner corners* – These are handled differently from outer corners. First strengthen the inner corner on the main fabric by stitching ⅝ in (1.5 cm) either side of the corner along the seam line. Clip into the corner, clipping close to the stitching (diagram 4).

  Stitch the binding to the fabric as before until you reach the corner. Stop with the needle down and the presser foot raised and open out the fabric beneath the binding at the clipped corner to form a straight line. Continue applying the binding. Bring the corner back together, folding the excess binding diagonally in the corner when turning the binding to the underside. Repeat on the underside, and again tuck the excess into a diagonal fold.

Diagram 3: Outer corner

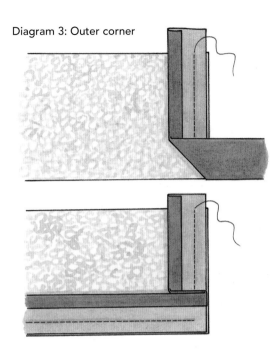

Diagram 4: Inner corner

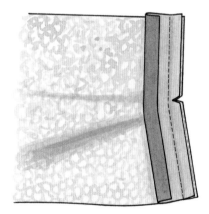

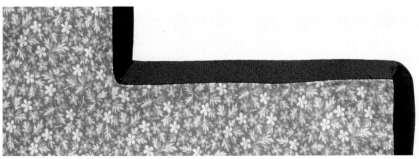

Bound corners

PIPING

Piping is a corded trim, which can be plain cord covered with fabric or decorative cord with a tape that is sewn between the fabric layers so the piping sits on the edge. It is used on soft furnishings and customized clothing. Piping cord varies in thickness, thicker cords being used for heavyweight furnishings and finer cord for fashion.

Fabric-covered piping – As with bias tape, the fabric to cover piping cord needs to be cut on the bias, approximately 1 in (2.5 cm) wide and as long as required (join lengths if necessary). Fold the strips in half lengthwise, wrong sides together and with the cord sandwiched within the fold, machine stitch the edges together.

Decorative piping – This comes attached to a flange or tape which helps to hold the piping in place by being stitched within the seam allowance. Again, there are different widths of cord for different applications.

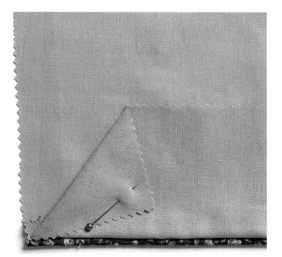

Piped edge

General sewing tips

- Use the inseam method of insertion. Pin the piping to the right side of one piece of the main fabric, matching the raw edge of the fabric and the tape (diagram 5).
- Use a zipper foot to stitch the cord in place.
- Add a second piece of fabric, right sides and edges matching, and then stitch again, stitching as close to the cord as possible. Trim, clip, and notch the seam allowances before turning through. The piping is now neatly on the outer edge.

Overlapping piping ends

Fabric-covered piping – Pin the piping to the fabric as above, then where the ends are to overlap, open the piping fabric and on the under piece, turn the raw end to the inside. Trim the piping cord back 1 in (2.5 cm). Lay the other end of the piping fabric over the first with the cord ends meeting (if desired, hand stitch the cord ends together) (diagram 6). Fold the piping cord again and stitch in place. Add the second layer of fabric as before.

Decorative piping – Start with the piping off the edge of the fabric (starting in an inconspicuous area), curving it onto the seam line and attaching as before. When the piping is to overlap, again curve off the fabric edge over the beginning (diagram 7). It may be necessary to make the last stitches one at a time or by hand as the trim and fabric together are very bulky.

Diagram 5: Inseam method of insertion

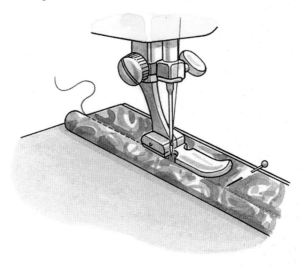

Diagram 6: Fabric-covered piping

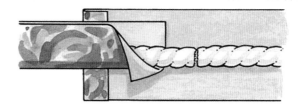

Diagram 7: Decorative piping

SURFACE TRIMS

These are trims that are added to the surface of a project and can be applied by hand or machine. If the trim is over ½ in (13 mm) wide, it is advisable to stitch down both long edges, stitching both in the same direction. Choose a thread that matches the trim.

Diagram 8: Mitering corners

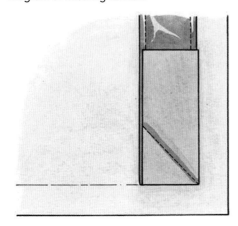

Mitering at corners

Stitch the trim in place down both long edges, ending the stitching at the seam line at the corner. Fold the trim back on itself and then again along the new stitching line (as for binding corners). Press.

Unfold the trim so it is just back on itself again and stitch along the diagonal crease (diagram 8). If using a bulky trim, cut away the excess under the diagonal stitching. Fold the trim back along the second placement line again and continue stitching along both long edges.

BEADED TRIMS

Trims with beading are used as decorative embellishment for furnishings, craft projects, and fashions. Again the beading is attached to a tape, which can be encased within seam allowances (as piping) or stitched to the surface. If stitched within the seam, remove any beads in the seam allowance by crushing them.

To create curved corners, clip into the tape at the corners, bending it around the corner (diagram 9). Use a zipper foot to stitch close to the beading.

Selection of beaded trims

Diagram 9: Curved corner

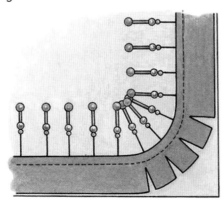

HELPFUL HINT:
If beading is long, temporarily hold it against the main fabric with masking tape so the beads don't get caught in the stitching.

FRINGE

As with beaded trims or piping, fringe can be added inseam if it has a tape attached, or as a surface trim.

Self-fringe can also be created by cutting into fabrics that don't fray easily. Decide on the depth of fringe desired and then stitch a guide line. Cut up to this line at even intervals. This type of fringe is ideal on fleece fabrics or bias-cut fabrics that will not unravel.

Selection of fringes

ELASTIC AND CASINGS

Elastic comes in many widths and styles, each for a different purpose. These include regular straight-edged elastic available in a range of widths, lingerie elastic that can be clear or have decorative edges, fine elastic thread or cord, tubular elastic through which cord can be threaded (for swimwear), buttonhole elastic – with evenly spaced buttonholes, sportswear elastic and waistbanding.

Elastic can be inserted into a tunnel (casing), applied to the right side of a waist and turned to the inside, or applied at the same time as a casing is formed. Lingerie elastic is designed to be seen and thus is added to the edges.

Types of elastic

HELPFUL HINT:
To avoid difficulty feeding elastic through a casing when it comes up against seams, before stitching the casing, use a little fusible hem web to stick the seam allowances down.

Casing with elastic in

EASY CASINGS

Used on waists, trouser legs, or sleeve hems, casings are created as tunnels through which the elastic is threaded. When cutting out garment sections, remember to add approximately 2 in (5 cm) for the casing (commercial patterns will include an extension to the pattern piece).

1. Having stitched the side seams of the garment, finish the raw edge of the casing section before turning to the inside. Pin in place and machine stitch close to the inner fold, leaving a gap of about 1½ in (4 cm) for elastic insertion (diagram 1). Stitch around the casing again, this time close to the top fold. Make sure the space between the rows of stitching is wide enough for the width of elastic.

2. Determine the length of the elastic by measuring around the body at waist/sleeve/ trouser hem. Subtract 1 in (2.5 cm) from this measurement.

Diagram 1: Finish the raw edge of the casing

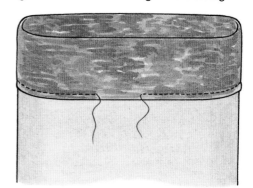

3. Using a safety pin, thread the elastic through the casing and out again at the same place. Overlap the elastic ends and machine stitch them together before allowing them to disappear inside the casing. Before stitching the ends together, pin with a safety pin and try the garment on for size.

Diagram 2: Adjust the gathers equally

 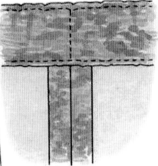

HELPFUL HINT:
To prevent the other end of the elastic disappearing inside the casing as you thread it through, anchor it to the garment with another safety pin.

4. Finish by adjusting the gathers equally and then machine stitching from the top edge to the bottom of the casing at the side seams, center back, and center front (this will also help prevent the elastic twisting within the casing) (diagram 2).

APPLIED CASING

Another form of casing, applied casing is used on dresses at the waist, on shaped edges, or on heavyweight fabrics where a self-facing would be too bulky. Usually made from bias binding or seam binding tape, they are attached to the inside of the garment along both long edges. Ensure the two rows of stitching are far enough apart for the elastic width to sit flat.

To determine the length of bias tape, measure around the ungathered garment. Add ½ in (13 mm) for the seams. Pin in position, overlapping the ends. If necessary tuck the raw edge of the top overlap under. Insert the elastic where the tape overlaps.

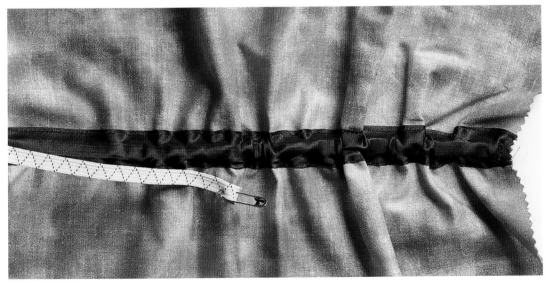

Applied casing

Diagram 3: Pin the elastic

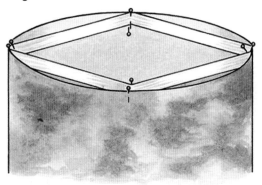

DIRECT APPLICATION

Used on shorts, sportswear, and knitted garments, the elastic is stitched to the top edge of fabric, which is then folded to the inside to form the casing. It is best applied using the "quartering" method.

1. Having determined the length of elastic needed, overlap and machine stitch the ends together to form a continuous piece.
2. Finish the top edge of the fabric and then divide into four equal parts (side seams, center front, and back). Divide the elastic into four equal parts also.
3. Pin the elastic at the matching quarter marks to the wrong side of the garment with one edge of elastic butted up to the finished garment edge (diagram 3).
4. Zigzag stitch the elastic to the garment, starting at one quarter mark and stretching the elastic to fit between quarter marks.
5. Fold the garment edge to the inside, taking the elastic with it and again pin in place at the quarter marks. Finish with zigzag stitch through all the layers close to the inner edge, stretching the elastic to fit between the quarters as before.

LINGERIE ELASTIC

Designed to be seen, this is applied to the finished edge of a garment, either on top or underneath the edge, again using the quartering method.

Stitching elastic with zigzag stitch to the wrong side of the top edge

STRAPS AND TIES

As the name suggests, straps and ties are used to tie or strap a garment and hold it in position. Straps are wider and ties tend to be narrow. They can be made from self-fabric, contrasting fabric, or ribbons and braids.

GENERAL SEWING TIPS

- For waist ties, cut fabric strips on the bias to provide extra stretch. For halter neck or shoulder straps, cut fabric on the straight of grain to prevent unwanted stretch.
- Interface straps made of lightweight fabric to add stability.
- Fold the strap or tie in half lengthwise, with right sides together and machine stitch the long edge. Turn through to the right side and

reposition the seam at the center back. Press (diagram 1).

Diagram 1: Fold, stitch, and turn through

Garment top with straps and ties

Diagram 2: Spaghetti strap

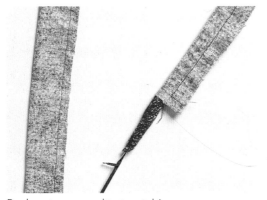

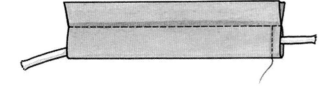

Rouleau turner used to turn tubing

Diagram 3: Cord method

- If you are working with very long straps, machine stitch the short ends and then pivot and stitch the long side, leaving a turning gap in the center of the long edge. Trim the seam allowances and corners at an angle and turn through. Slip stitch the opening closed.
- To make rounded spaghetti straps, do not trim the seam allowance after stitching, turn through and allow the seam allowance to fill the tube (diagram 2).
- Use a rouleau turner (long, thin needlelike tool with a fine hook on one end) to turn through very thin ties.
- An alternative method of stitching and turning a strap or tie easily is to use the cord method. Anchor a long cord at one end and sandwich between the folded fabric, with the cord close to the fold. Allow enough cord to leave a 5 in (13 cm) tail. Machine stitch the long edge, without stitching into the cord. Pull on the cord to pull through the tubing. Cut off the cord and keep for later use (diagram 3).
- Stitch the straps to the right side of the garment prior to adding the facings, matching the end of the strap with the garment edge. Before attaching straps at the back of a garment, pin in place and try the garment on to check the strap length.
- For halter neck ties, simply knot the free end.

APPLIQUÉ

Applying patches or motifs to the fabric surface adds interest, can liven up plain projects, or cover worn areas. The term *appliqué* is used to describe the decorative patches as well as the method of attaching them.

Often used as a finishing touch, there are different types of appliqué. The most commonly used methods are dealt with here – plain, reverse, and raw edge. Others include "Mola," where multiple layers of different colored fabrics are cut through at different levels to create colorful pictures, and "Shadow," which involves adding appliqué shapes under layers of sheer fabric.

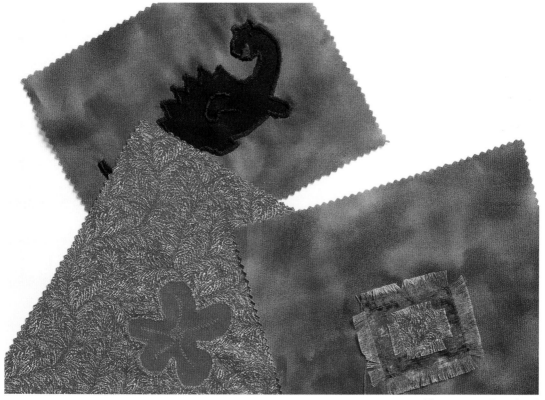

Three types of appliqué

General sewing tips

- Appliqué shapes can be cut from contrast fabric, from printed motifs on print fabrics, or be ready-made. They are usually stitched in place with satin stitch (very close zigzag stitch, width 3, length 0.45), or if appliqué fabric doesn't ravel, use a blanket or straight stitch.

- Keep the motif in position while stitching by bonding with fusible web or temporary craft glue.
- If appliquéing onto lightweight fabrics, support the area to prevent the fabric puckering when densely stitched by adding a layer of tearaway stabilizer, which is then torn away once stitching

Diagram 1: Number appliqués

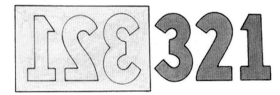

Diagram 2: Satin stitch the visible layers

is complete (see interfacings and stabilizers, page 39).

- When adding lettering or numbers, take care to ensure they are the right way round. If drawn on the reverse of the appliqué fabric first, they will need to be back to front so when turned over, they are read correctly (diagram 1).

- Stitch slowly to control the direction. The stitch on the right swing of the needle is on the main fabric and the left swing on the appliqué. At curves and corners, stop with the needle down – on inner curves, with the needle in the appliqué; on outer curves, with the needle in the main fabric – then pivot the work slightly before continuing.

- Use a thread color to match the appliqué. If you are making a multi-layered appliqué, hand baste the different layers in place and then satin stitch the top of visible layers only, again with threads to match the appliqué fabric, unless a contrast is desired (diagram 2).

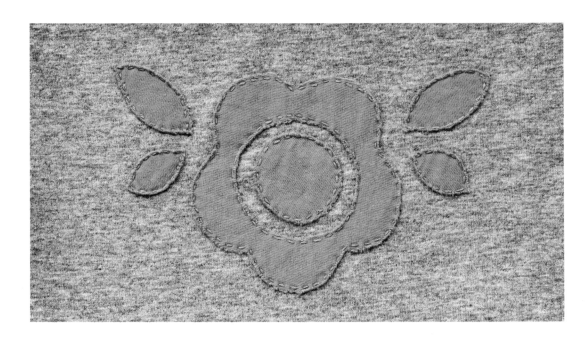

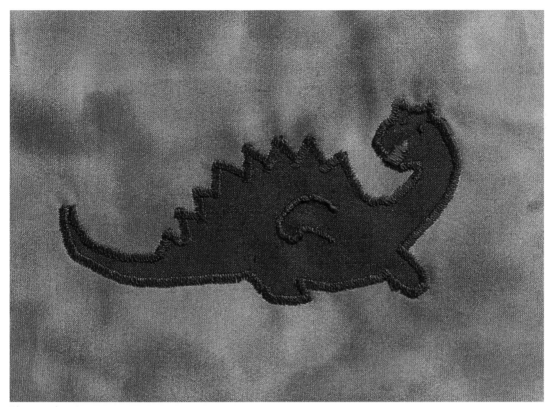

Plain appliqué

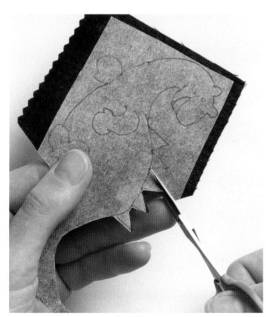

Cutting out appliqué fused with paper-backed fusible webbing

PLAIN APPLIQUÉ

This is the most common appliqué technique and is used to create pictures or add motifs. The motifs or components of a picture can be cut from any compatible fabric.

Use paper-backed fusible webbing to anchor the appliqué to the main fabric. First apply the fusible side to the reverse of a piece of appliqué fabric. Then draw around the design and cut out accurately. Remove the paper backing and fuse to the right side of the main garment.

Stitch the appliqué in place using satin stitch, which will also cover the raw edges.

RAW EDGE APPLIQUÉ

As the name suggests, the edges of the applied fabric are left raw to fray and fluff up or be fringed. The appliqué fabric must be cut square or in line with the fabric weave if it is to be fringed (check by pulling thread from the side edges both horizontally and vertically). Fuse the appliqué in place as before, but with fusible web that is ⅝ in (1.5 cm) smaller all around so the edges are not fused. Stitch in place with straight or decorative stitch, ⅝ in (1.5 cm) from the edge. Press and then fringe by pulling out threads from the sides.

HELPFUL HINT:
Leave the raw edges unfringed and wash repeatedly to get a casual, fluffy edge or pink with pinking shears.

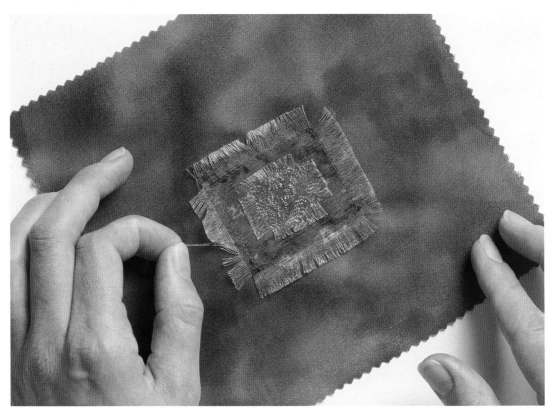

Pulling threads from raw edge appliqué

REVERSE APPLIQUÉ

The appliqué fabric is applied to the back of the work and then the main fabric is cut away within the design area before being satin stitched around the edges. The result is similar to plain appliqué, but with the motif being lower rather than raised from the main fabric. A combination of the two methods produces a textural 3D piece of work.

Working on the wrong side of the main fabric, fuse interfacing to the area to be appliquéd. Add the appliqué fabric, right side toward the interfacing. Draw the design on the appliqué fabric in reverse and then straight stitch around the design (diagram 3).

Turn the work to the right side and cut away the main fabric within and close to the stitching. Satin stitch or narrow zigzag stitch around the raw edges. Finish by trimming away the excess appliqué fabric from the reverse of the work.

Reverse 3D appliqué

Diagram 3: Straight stitch around the design

MAKING CURTAINS AND BLINDS

Sewing for the home has become more and more popular, as rooms can be revamped with a selection of easily made curtains and blinds. Using beautiful furnishing fabrics in a range of colors and styles can make all the difference between plain curtains and sumptuous window treatments.

WINDOW TREATMENTS

The first consideration is what type of window treatment will suit your room. Is the window large or small? Do you want curtains that are full length, or finish on or just below the windowsill (diagram 1)?

Would a blind be a better option? The hardware is another consideration – curtain tracks or poles? These need to be in place, or the placement marked, before measurements can be accurately taken.

Diagram 1: Curtain lengths

CALCULATING FABRIC AMOUNTS

Length

Having decided on the length of curtain – floor length (½ in/13 mm from floor), below sill length (3 in/8 cm below sill), or on sill – take the measurements from the top of the pole or track to the hem length. At the moment this measurement does not include header and hem allowance (diagram 2).

Width

Measure from the outer edges of the brackets on the pole or track. Allow extra width on tracks that overlap at the center (diagram 2). *Note: if the window is close to the corner of the room also measure from the window to the corner. If less than 8 in (20 cm), there won't be adequate room between the wall and the window to open the curtains properly, so consider one curtain hung from the other side.*

Diagram 2: Measurements for fabric

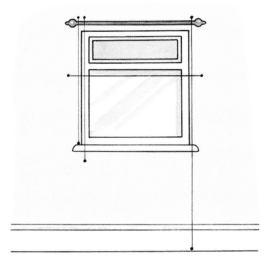

Curtain fullness

The amount of fullness is determined by the weight of fabric, as well as the type of header tape. For instance, deep pencil pleats require 3–3½ times fabric width to get the right fullness, whereas goblet-pleated headers need just 2¼ times fabric fullness.

As a general rule: heavy fabrics require a fullness factor of at least 2 to 1; medium-weight fabrics use a fullness factor of 2½ to 1; and lightweight fabrics or voiles look best with at least 3 to 1.

HELPFUL HINT:
If you don't know the depth of the header tape you wish to use, err on the side of caution and allow 8 in (20 cm).

Joining lengths or panels

In order to make up the total width required, it may be necessary to join lengths or panels of fabrics together. When calculating requirements, round up to the nearest inch/cm. For instance, if the window is 87 in (220 cm) wide and you want 2¼ times fullness, that is 196 in (495 cm), which will be divided into two curtains of 98 in (248 cm). If the fabric width is 54 in (140 cm), to get the width needed for each curtain will require approximately 1.8 panels joined together for each curtain – rounded up to 2 panels per curtain (which also allows a little for side hems and seams joining panels).

Header tapes, hems, and pattern repeats

Other factors to consider before calculating how much fabric is needed include pattern repeat on the chosen fabric, which header tape you wish to use, and how deep the hem should be. The pattern repeat is the amount of fabric that a recurring pattern or design on the fabric takes up before it is repeated again (diagram 3). Sometimes you may need to measure the pattern repeat on a length in the shop; others will note the repeat on the ticket. You will need to add the pattern repeat amount to every length of fabric required to make up the width of each curtain.

Header tape – Add double the depth of the header tape (this can vary from 1–8 in/2.5–20 cm). A goblet header tape is 4 in (10 cm) deep, so 8 in (20 cm) is added to the length. The amount of header tape needed is the same as the overall width, plus 6 in (15 cm) for turnings.

Hem allowance – Longer, heavier curtains look better with a wider hem of 4 in (10 cm), lightweight and shorter curtains can have a narrower hem of 2 in (5 cm). Add double the hem depth to each curtain length.

Pattern repeat – As mentioned above, to each length/panel you need to add the pattern repeat of the design on the fabric so that when panels are joined, the pattern matches across the width. For example, a pattern repeat of 13 in (33 cm) needs to be added to each length that makes up one curtain.

Diagram 3: Pattern repeat

To calculate your own requirements complete this simple chart:

Length:
Window length from pole to hem line
Plus header tape depth x 2
Plus hem depth x 2
Plus pattern repeat
= total length per panel
Width:
Window width from pole (outer bracket to outer bracket) plus overlap if curtains overlap
Multiplied by fullness required, i.e. 2, 2½, 3 or 3½ (determined by header type or fabric thickness) =
Divide this by the number of curtains (thus total width per curtain)
Divide this by width of fabric to calculate how many lengths

LININGS

Linings add weight to curtains and help them hang better. They also provide added insulation against cold and light, cut down the noise and dust that filters through a window, and give a uniform appearance from the outside.

There are two types of lining: sewn-in (the most commonly used) and loose linings that have a special lining header tape that is attached to the main curtains with hooks. For loose linings you need approximately 1½ times the window width. Sew them in the same way as main curtains.

Sewn-in linings require the same fullness of fabric as the main fabric. The only difference in the calculations is there is no need to add pattern repeat.

Normally curtain lining is white or off-white cotton sateen. However, sheeting, unbleached muslin gauze, or pretty cotton prints can also be used. Consider using a pretty cotton if the underside may be visible when curtains are tied back.

PELMETS, VALENCES, SWAGS, AND JABOTS

These are treatments for dressing the top of a window that can be used in conjunction with or instead of curtains.

Pelmets or cornices – These are hardwood boxes, which can be shaped, covered in fabric, and trimmed to match the curtains (diagram 4).

Valances – These are soft fabric toppers like mini curtains, often in a matching or co-ordinating fabric to the main curtains (diagram 5). They can be finished with the same header tape or a more intricate tape. Both pelmets and valances will cover the tops of the curtains.

Swags and jabots – A classic swag is a draping of soft fabric folds used as a top treatment with pleated or gathered side panels. The side panels are the jabots, also known as cascades or tails (diagram 6).

Diagram 4: Pelmet or cornice

Diagram 5: Valance

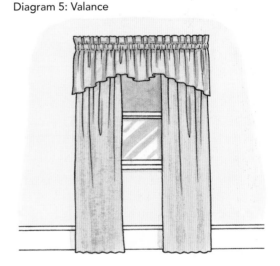

Diagram 6: Swag and jabots

DRAPERY HEADERS

There are a number of different options to finish the top of curtains. The most common is to add a header tape which is then gathered to form uniform pleats of some sort. Other options include eyelet curtains, tab top, and curtains with casings, all of which are threaded onto curtain poles.

Header tapes

These are usually white and have cords attached to the tape in a regular pattern, so that when pulled from one end, the tape and therefore curtain gather evenly. There is an extensive range of header tape styles to choose from.

Pencil pleat – Also known as Regis, this is the most popular type of header. For a full effect, you need 2–2½ times the fabric width with this type of tape so that when gathered, it produces evenly spaced pleats across the curtain. It is available in different widths, from narrow tape for lightweight or short curtains and voiles, to deeper tapes, ideal for heavier and full-length curtains. The deeper the tape, the fuller the pleats. Another option is a clear pencil pleat tape designed for transparent fabrics or a mini tape which is used for very lightweight gathers on sheer fabrics.

Pinch pleats – These come in a variety of pinch types, from Tridis to goblet. Tridis pleats are slightly more fanned rather than all even top to bottom, while goblet pleats quite literally resemble a goblet cup. Again the tape is created with cords, attached along the length so that when pulled up, the tape and curtain pleat in a regular design.

Press 'n' Drape – This is another useful product that is used to attach valances or curtains to unusually shaped frames. One part of the tape has hooks (similar to hook and loop tape) which will then "hook" on to the special dual-purpose header tapes that incorporate the loops.

Dual purpose box pleat – The term dual purpose means it can be used with the Press 'n' Drape window fitting or as a regular tape. The box pleat style provides a very crisp look. Other dual purpose tapes include Trellis and Smocked Pleats – again when cords are pulled up, the header tape gathers into a trellis or smocked style.

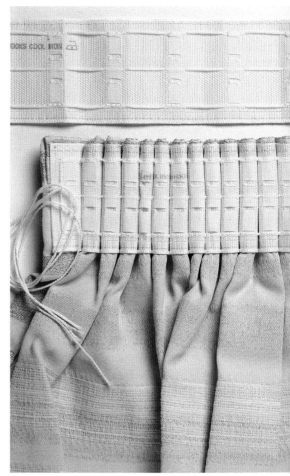

Pencil pleat header

Eyelet – Another option is to finish curtains with large eyelets, so that the curtain is threaded onto a pole. The tape is pre-printed with large circular holes or eyelets at even intervals. The tape is attached to the curtain top in the usual way, and then the eyelets are cut from the fabric. To finish off, large two-part rings, available in different metal finishes, are snapped into place front and back of the curtain covering the raw edges of the cut-outs.

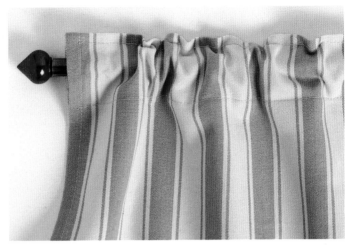

Casing curtain

Casing curtains – Also known as café curtains, these do not require header tape. Instead, a deep casing is created at the top of the curtain by turning the top edge to the underside, and stitching from side edge to side edge, approximately 3 in (8 cm) from the top and then again, 1 in (2.5 cm) from the top. The curtain is then slipped onto a rod (which is concealed within the casing). The amount of fabric width needed for this type of curtain depends on the length of the curtain, but can be as little as 1½ widths.

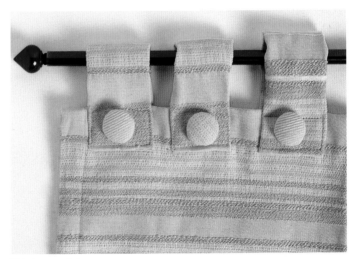

Tab top curtain

Tab top curtains – These curtains have fabric strips that are looped over a pole and attached to the curtain top by machine stitching or using buttons or clips. The width and intervals between the tab tops depend on curtain weight and length: the longer and heavier the curtains, the wider and closer the tabs need to be (to prevent the curtain sagging in between the tabs). As a guide, allow a gap of half the finished tab width between each tab. This type of curtain doesn't use as much fabric as curtains with headers as they are not usually gathered and thus are the width of the window plus turnings. The curtain top needs to be held above the window frame, so the pole may need to be positioned slightly higher than usual.

ADDING WEIGHTS

Hem weights are added to improve the hang of curtains, to give weight to the bottom, which in turn helps them hang straight. There are two main types of weight: a series of little lead pellets that are encased in a net tape, and round button-shaped disks that may have holes for sewing weights in place.

Lead tape – Lay the tape in the fold of the hem allowance, catch stitching it in place at the sides of the curtain.

Lead disks – Either stitch to the inside of the lining using the buttonholes or make little bags to hold the weights. To make the bags, simply cut a rectangle of fabric approximately ½ in (13 mm) wider than the disk by four times the disk size. Fold the fabric into thirds lengthwise, overlapping the center and then stitch the side seams together. Push the disk into the little bag and attach to the lining hem. Depending on the weight and length of the curtains, attach disks on either side or at intervals along the curtain bottom.

Weights

BLINDS

There are three main types of blind: Roman, Austrian, and roller. Blinds can be used instead of, or in addition to, curtains to dress a window. All will cover part of the window when up and thus may block a little light.

Roman blinds – This is the most common type of blind, which, when pulled up by drawstring cords, folds into neat, evenly spaced concertina folds held in place by rods inserted into pockets at the back of the blind (diagram 7). Longer blinds may have three or four center pleats, while smaller windows need just one or two. Each window will vary depending on the overall depth.

HELPFUL HINT:
Make the top pleat deeper and bottom pleat half width and the blind will fold up into equal pleats every time.

Austrian blinds – These are also pulled up by a cord system attached to the reverse of the blind. Preferably they should hang below a windowsill by about 10 in (25 cm), and the fabric needs to be twice the width of the batten, to which the blind is fixed at the top, to create the fullness. When down they look a bit like curtains, and when up, they gather into puffy swags (diagram 8). A lightweight fabric creates the best type of folds.

Roller blinds – These are the simplest style, with fabric rolled up onto a roller by a cord and sprocket system (diagram 9). Add an extra 8 in (20 cm) to the length so that there is some fabric on the roller when the blind is down. As the overall width of the roller itself is 1½ in (3.5 cm) wider than the fabric, make sure the fabric covers the glass completely.

Diagram 7: Roman blinds

Diagram 8: Austrian blinds

Diagram 9: Roller blinds

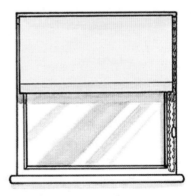

MEASURING FOR BLINDS

As blinds need to fit a window snugly, the first task is to measure accurately. The decision of whether to mount within the recess or outside depends on blind style, personal choice, and window openings (diagram 10).

Width – If the blind is to fit inside the recess, measure from side edge to side edge of the inner window frame. If it is to fit outside the recess, measure at least 3 in (8 cm) beyond the outer window frame to make sure the blind fully covers the recess. Measure the width at the top and bottom of the window in case it is not perfectly square or rectangular. Note: when fitting a blind inside the recess, attach the blind hardware at least 2 in (5 cm) in from the glass to prevent condensation damaging the blind.

Length – If the blind is to fit inside the recess, measure from the top of the hardware (wooden batten) to the sill. If it is to fit outside the recess, again measure from the top of the wooden batten to at least 2 in (5 cm) below the sill (or 10 in/25 cm for Austrian blinds).

Diagram 10: Measuring a window for blinds

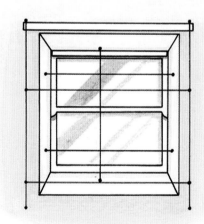

FABRIC REQUIRED

Add 2 in (5 cm) for seam allowances and hems to the window width measurement and 3½ in (9 cm) to the length. If necessary, join fabric widths to get the full width. For Austrian blinds, allow double the window width for the blind to gather effectively.

Both Austrian and Roman blinds also require lots of cording, blind tape, rod pockets, etc. The amount required will depend on the size of the blind. Kits are available which include all components. Alternatively, commercial patterns for blinds include details on how to measure and calculate requirements as well as a list of all the components needed.

INDEX

All images by IMM Lifestyle Books (photographer: Sian Irvine; illustrations: Coral Mula) except the following images by Shutterstock and their respective creators: 8th.creator (5 left, 54–55 top); Africa Studio (cover, 9, 124 bottom); Agnes Kantaruk (75 top); Alexey Smolyanyy (14 bottom left); Alkestida (hint box graphic throughout); Artush (171 bottom); bundit jonwises (37); Candus Camera (110 top); Cozy nook (5 stitches); David Pereiras (45); Dima Moroz (164); Ekaterina Garyuk (47 bottom left); EKramar (56–57, 65); Elena Elisseeva (70 top); EVGENIYA68 (51, 95, 106 top); Fotosoroka (14 top); grafvision (122 top); haris M (5 bottom, 10 bottom); HomeStudio (back cover left, 54–55 bottom); Jat306 (136–137 bottom); Katerina Maksymenko (144 top); Katvic (168 top); Kostikova Natalia (50 bottom, 98 top); kostolom3000 (inside covers, 1); kustomer (108–109 bottom); Larisa Lofitskaya (2); Lyudmila Suvorova (148 top); Maria Dryfhout (127 bottom); Mike Flippo (80–81 bottom); mtlapcevic (160 left); musicphone (103 top); Ortis (156 bottom); Pavel L Photo and Video (162 top); Perfect Lazybones (back cover right, 132 top); phive (8 left); photopia (102 bottom); Sergey Mironov (172); Sirtravelalot (170 top); studiovin (back cover bottom, 53 bottom, 112 bottom); Syda Productions (59 top, 66 bottom, 84–85, 96 bottom); Venus Angel (161 top); Vera Petrunina (118 bottom); veryulissa (6–7, 153 top); Vira Mylyan-Monastyrska (82 top); xiaorui (113 bottom); Yuriy Chertok (114 bottom); Zenobillis (27).